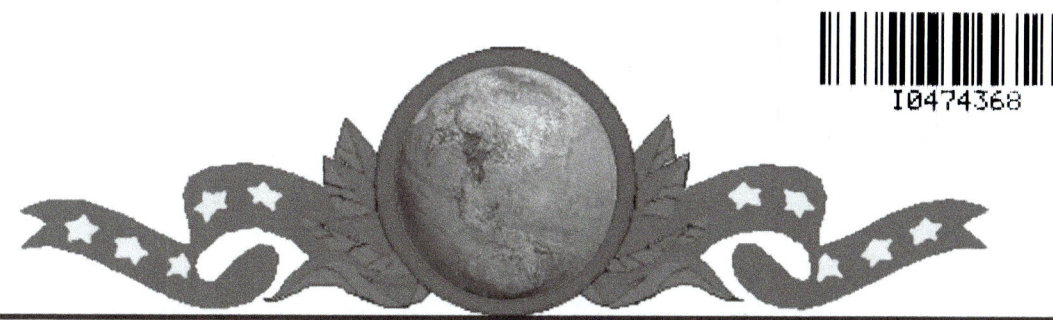

Real World
Colouring Book
For Advanced Users & Adults

Copyright 2019 By John Boom

50 Images

Created From Real Life Photos
For You To Colour As You Please.

ISBN 978-0-359-93602-1

90000

9 780359 936021

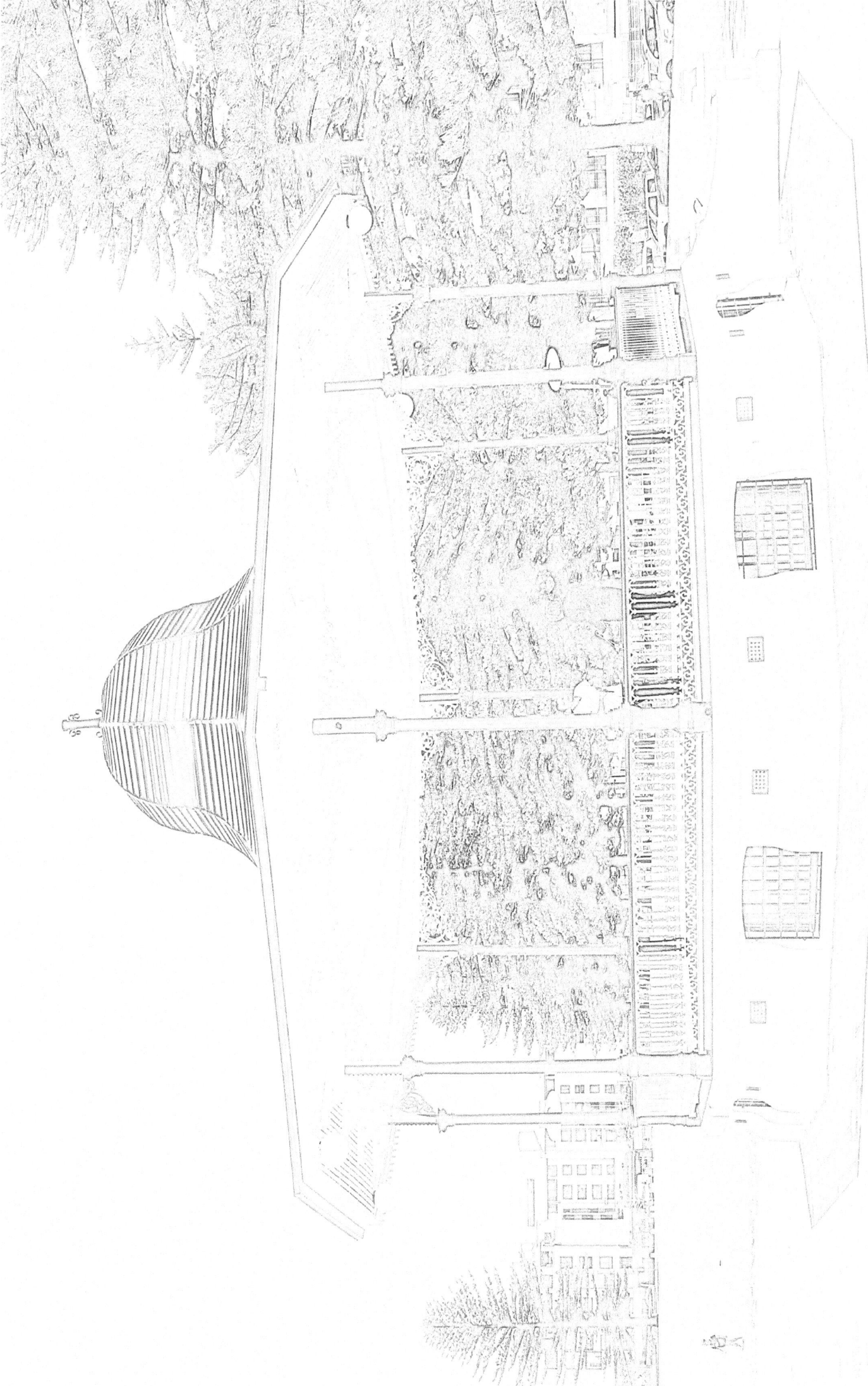

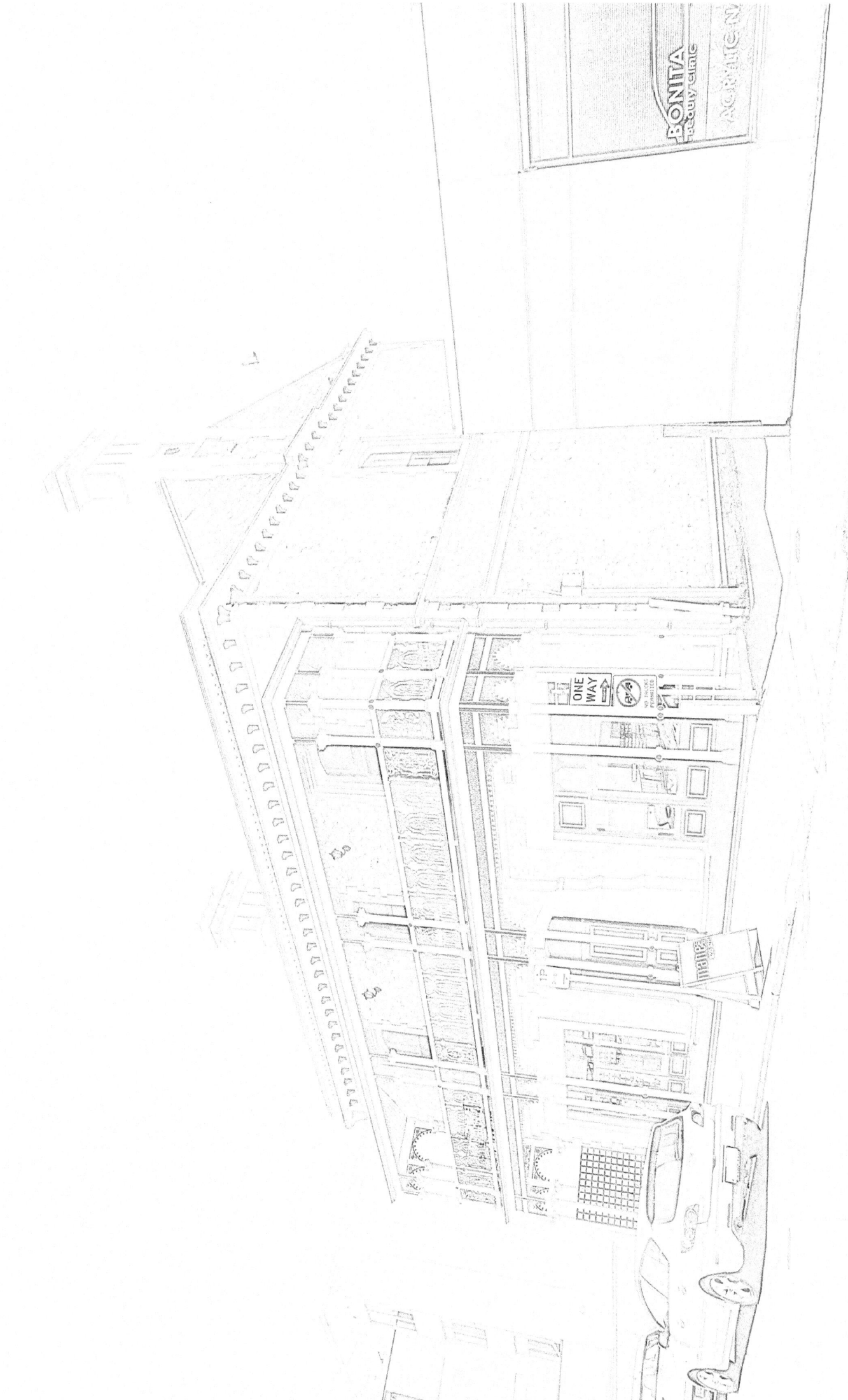

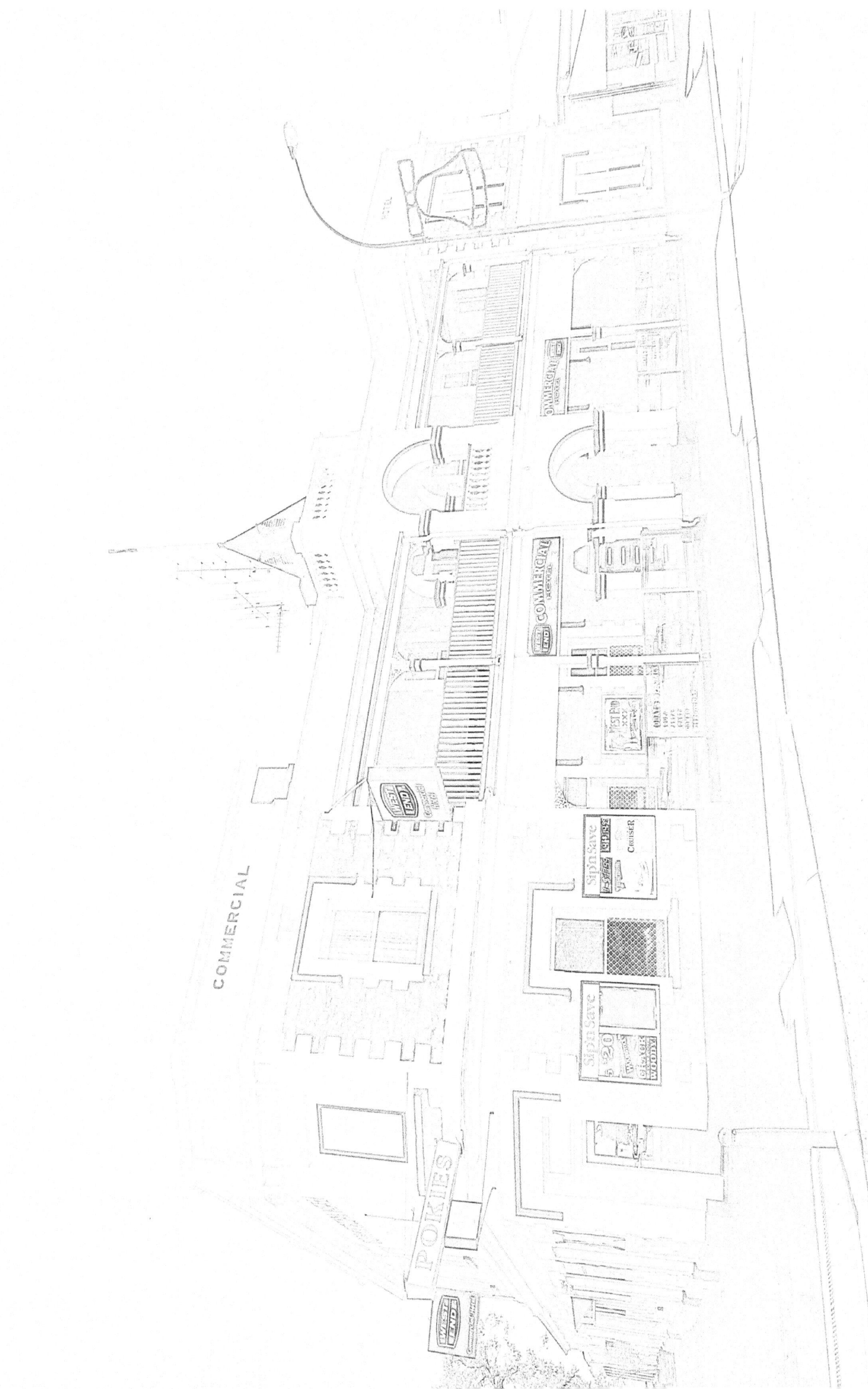

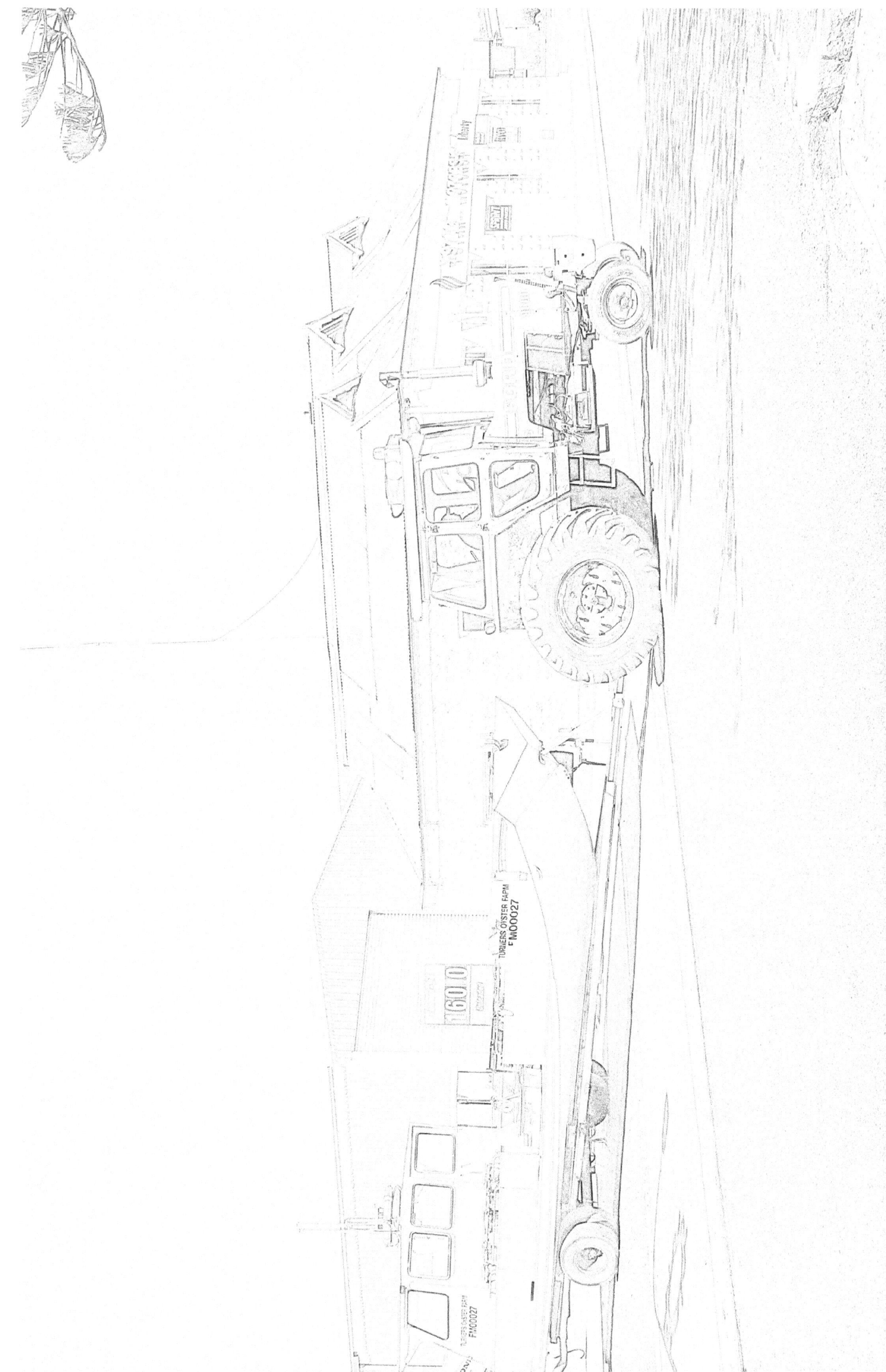

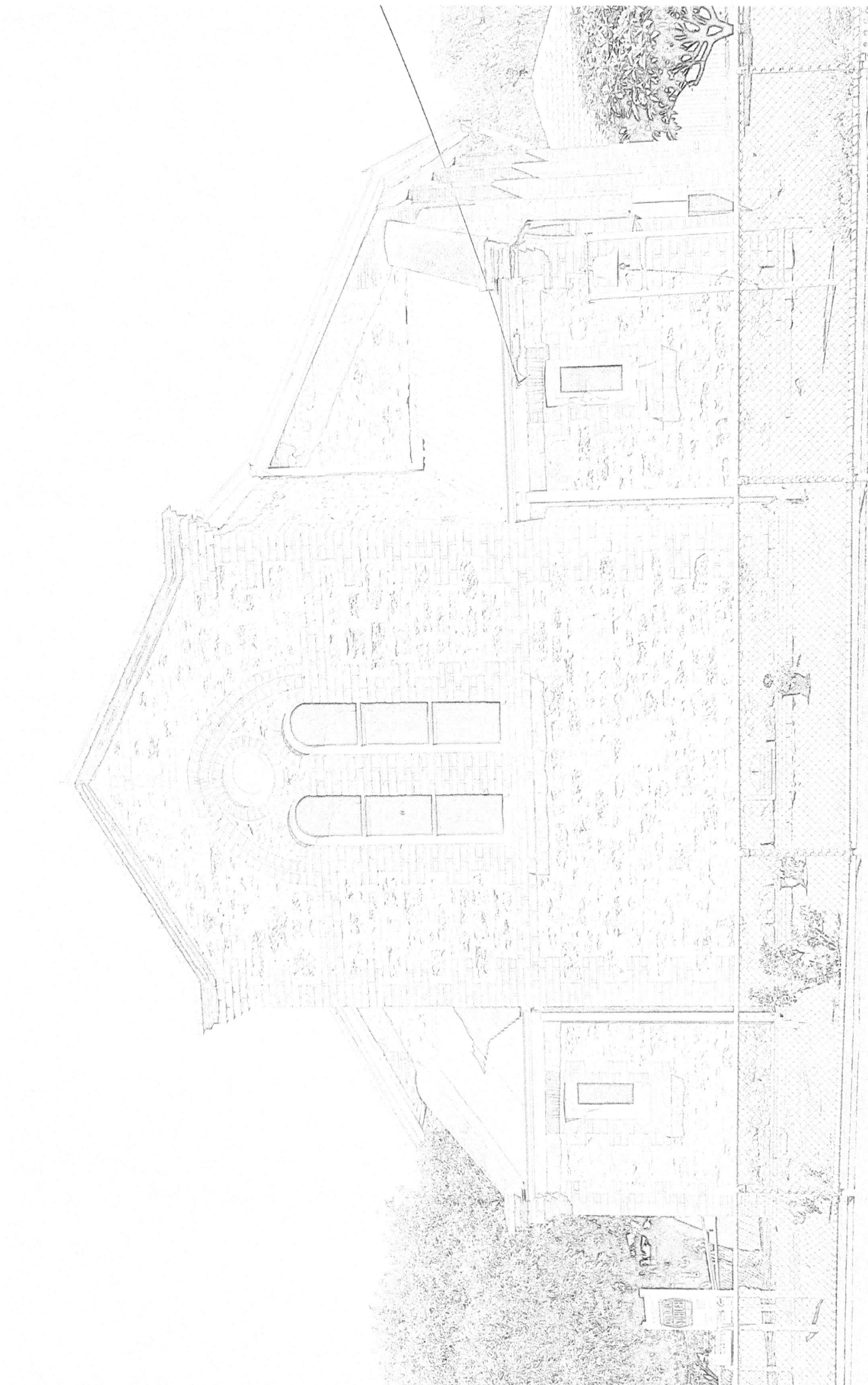

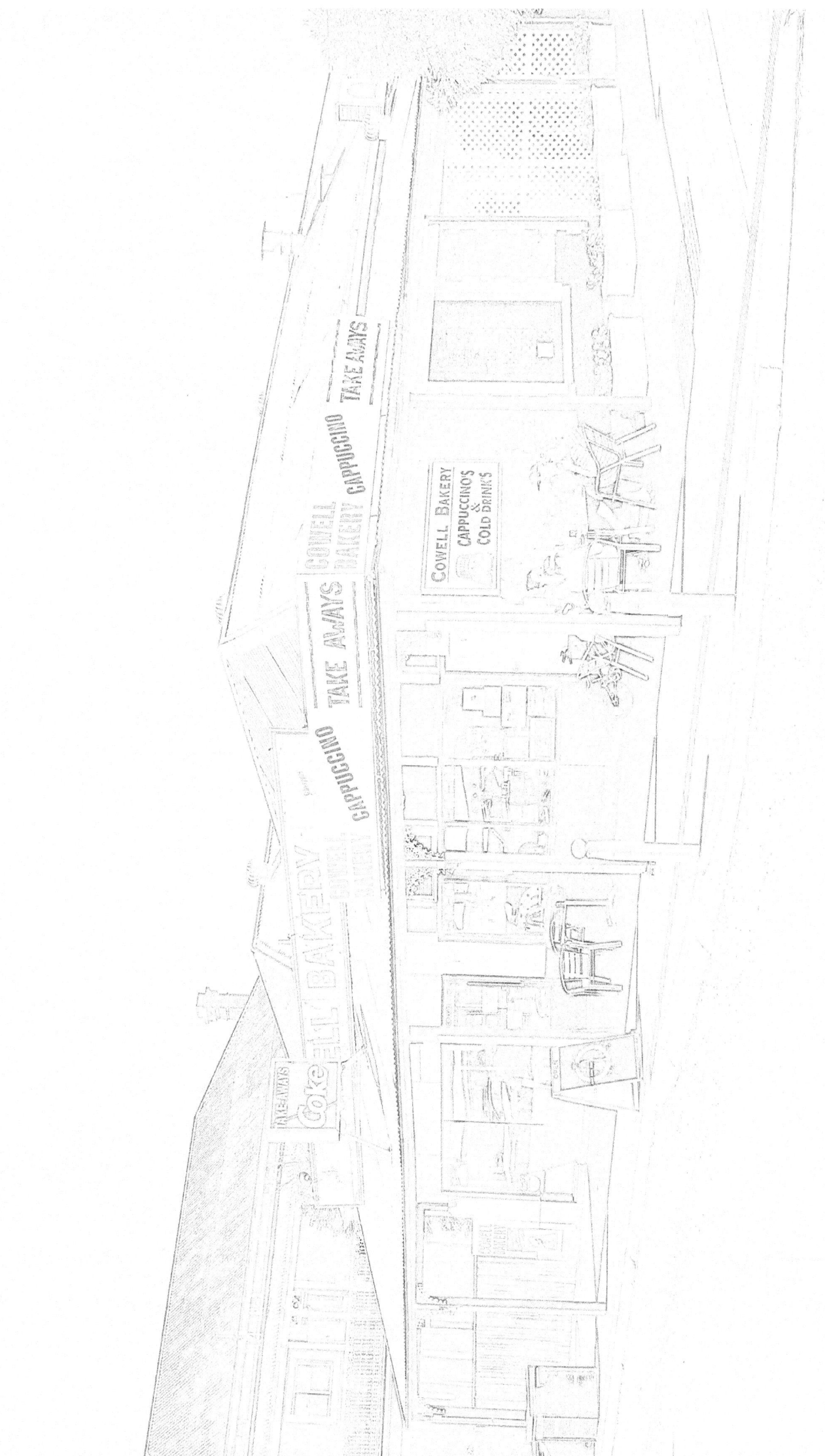

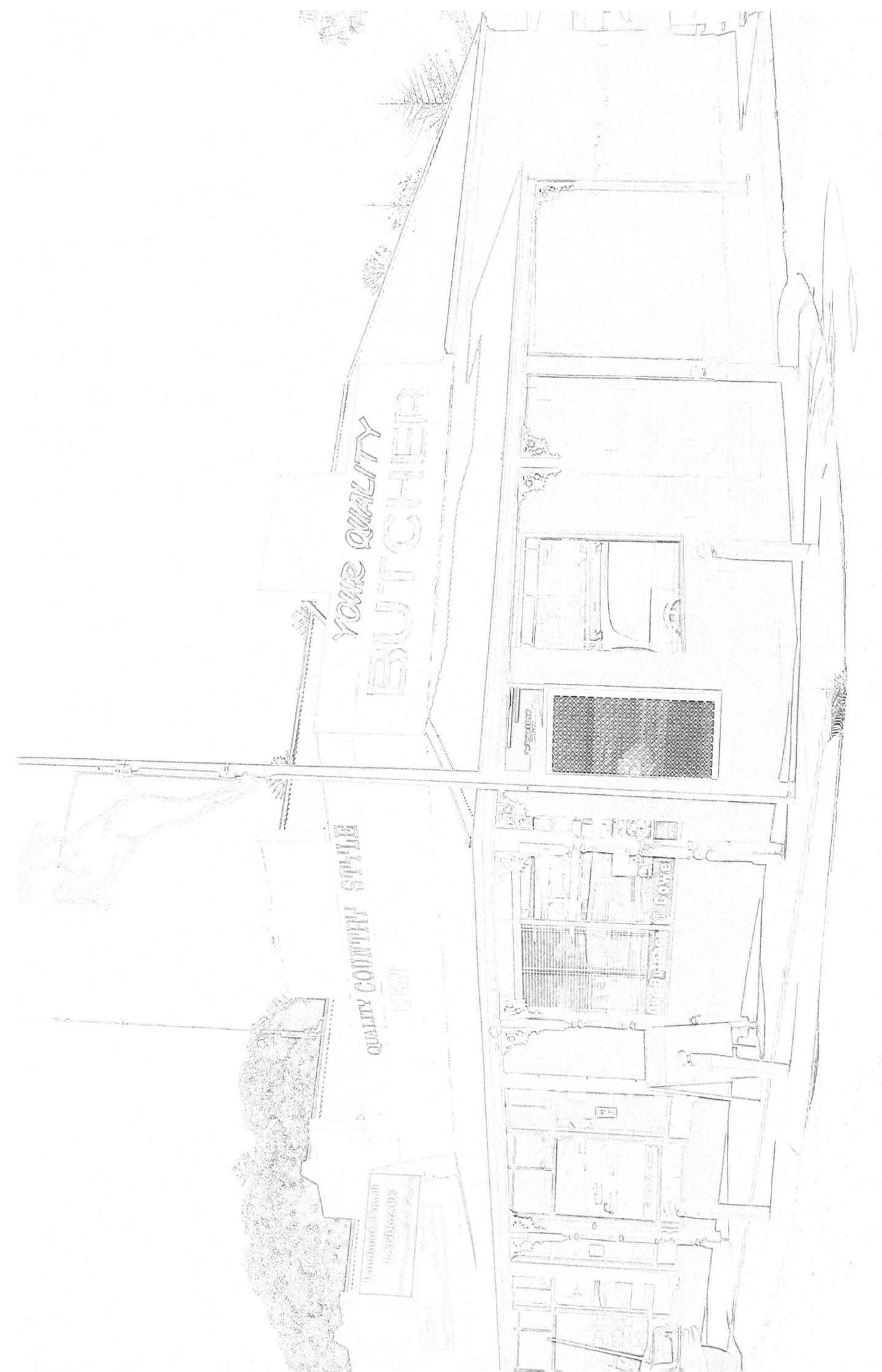

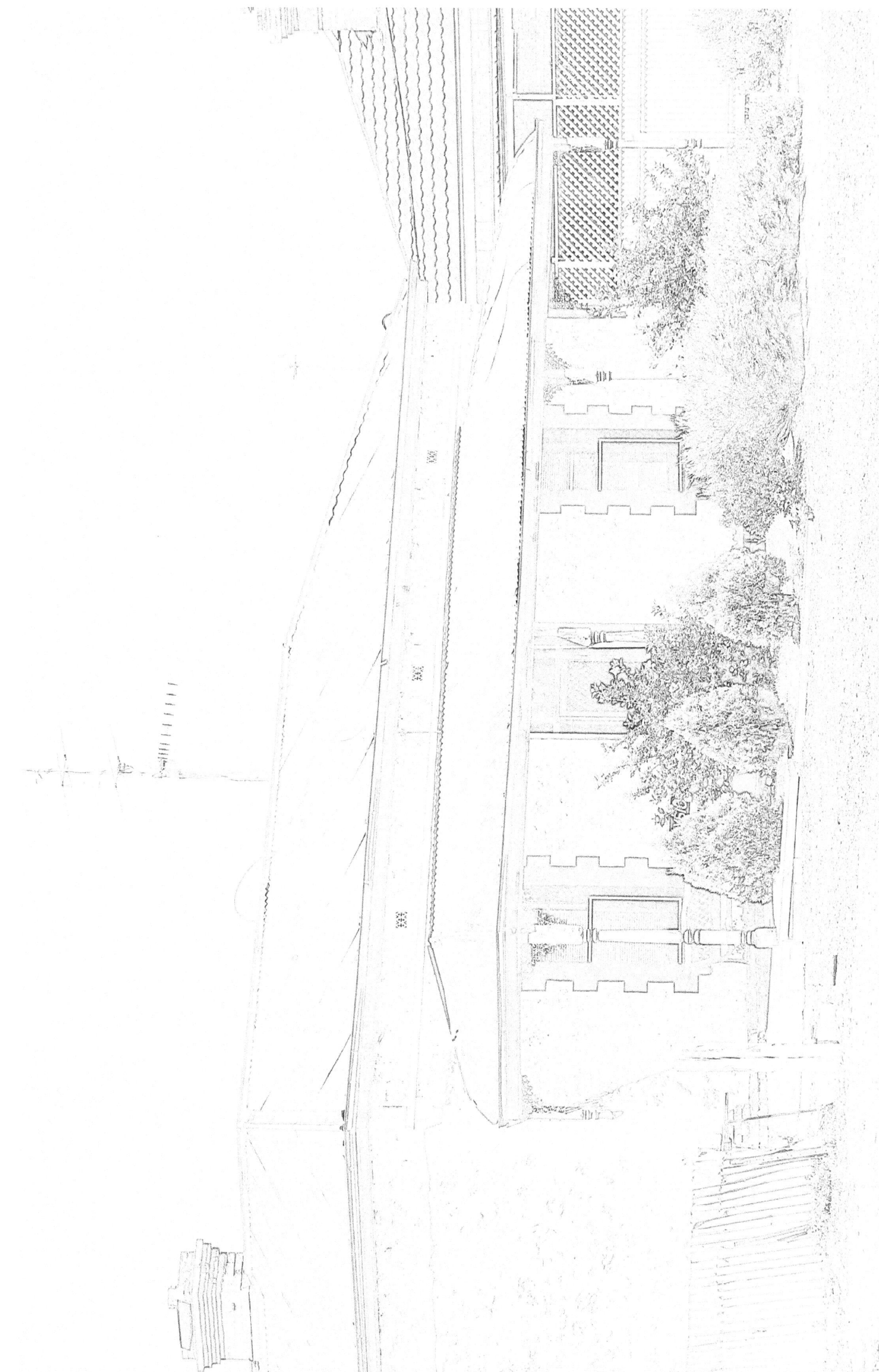

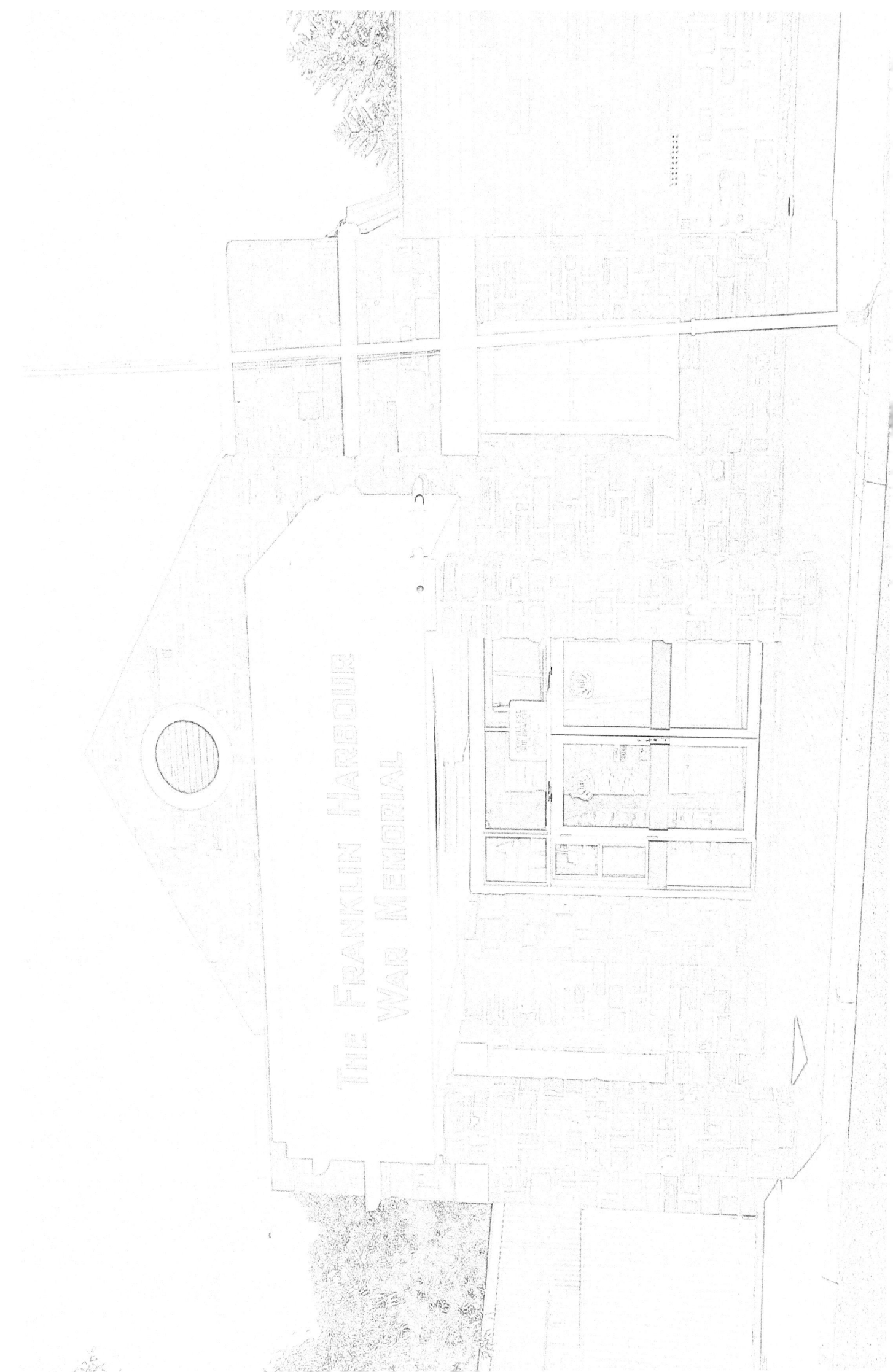

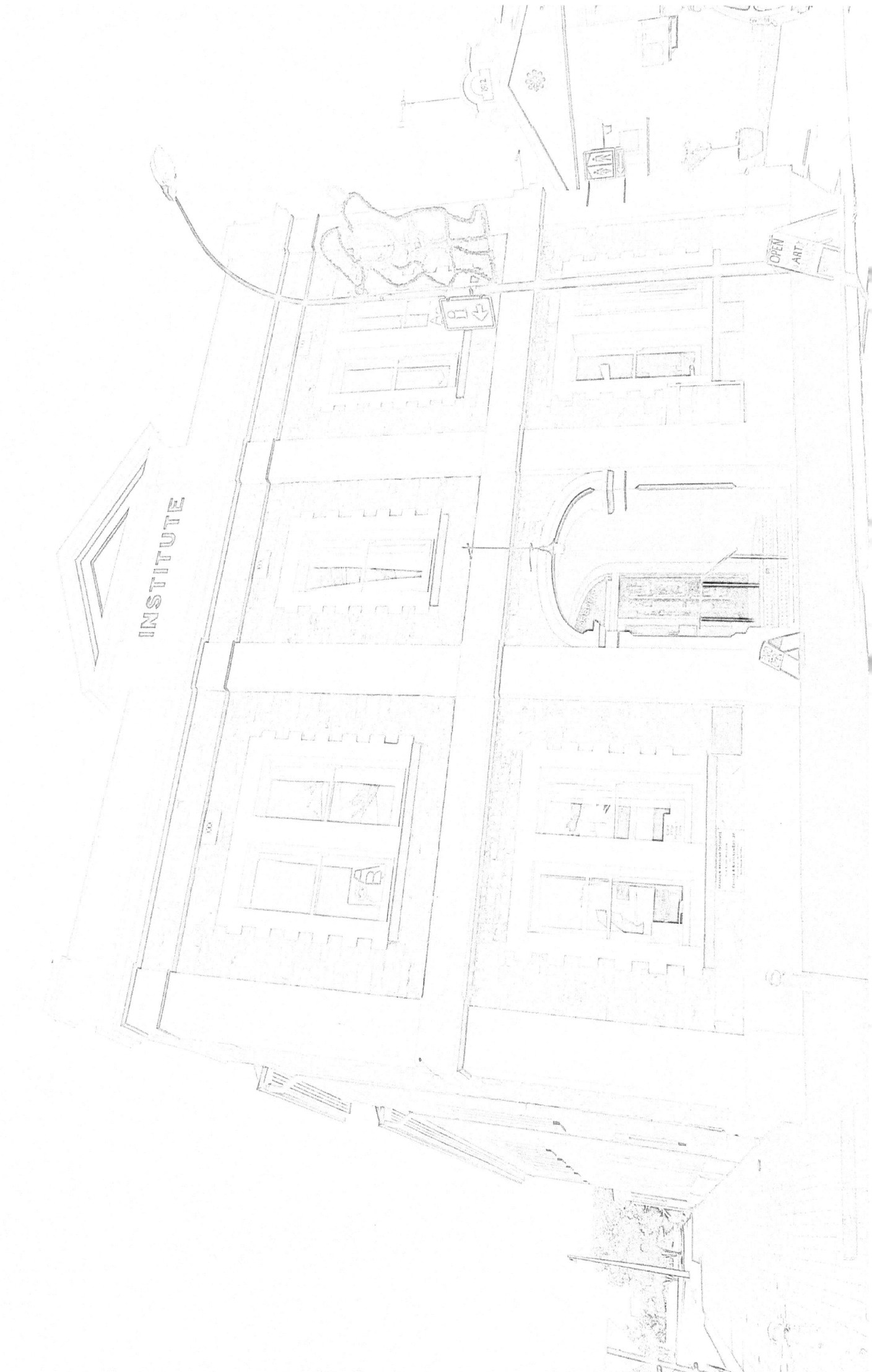

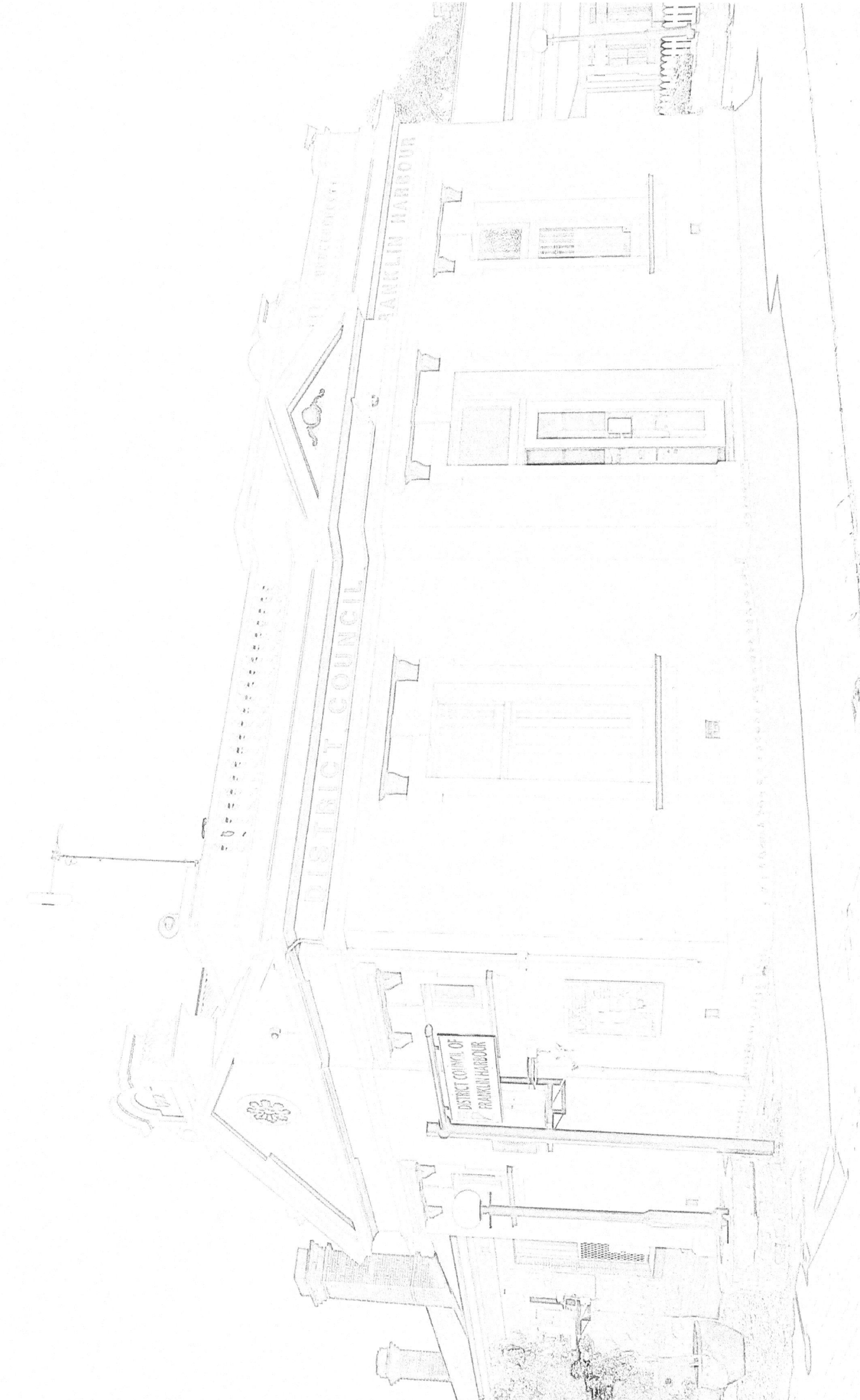

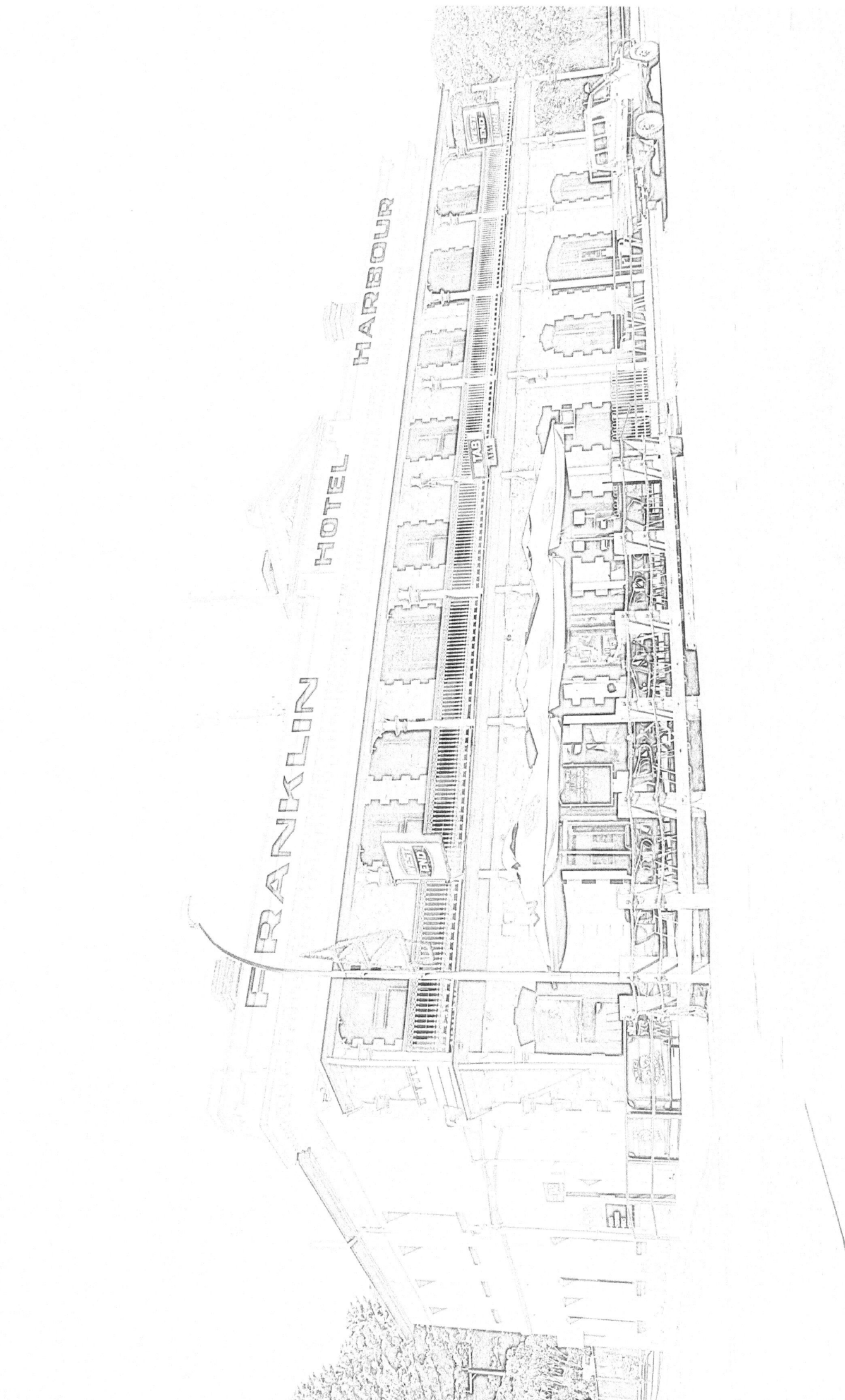

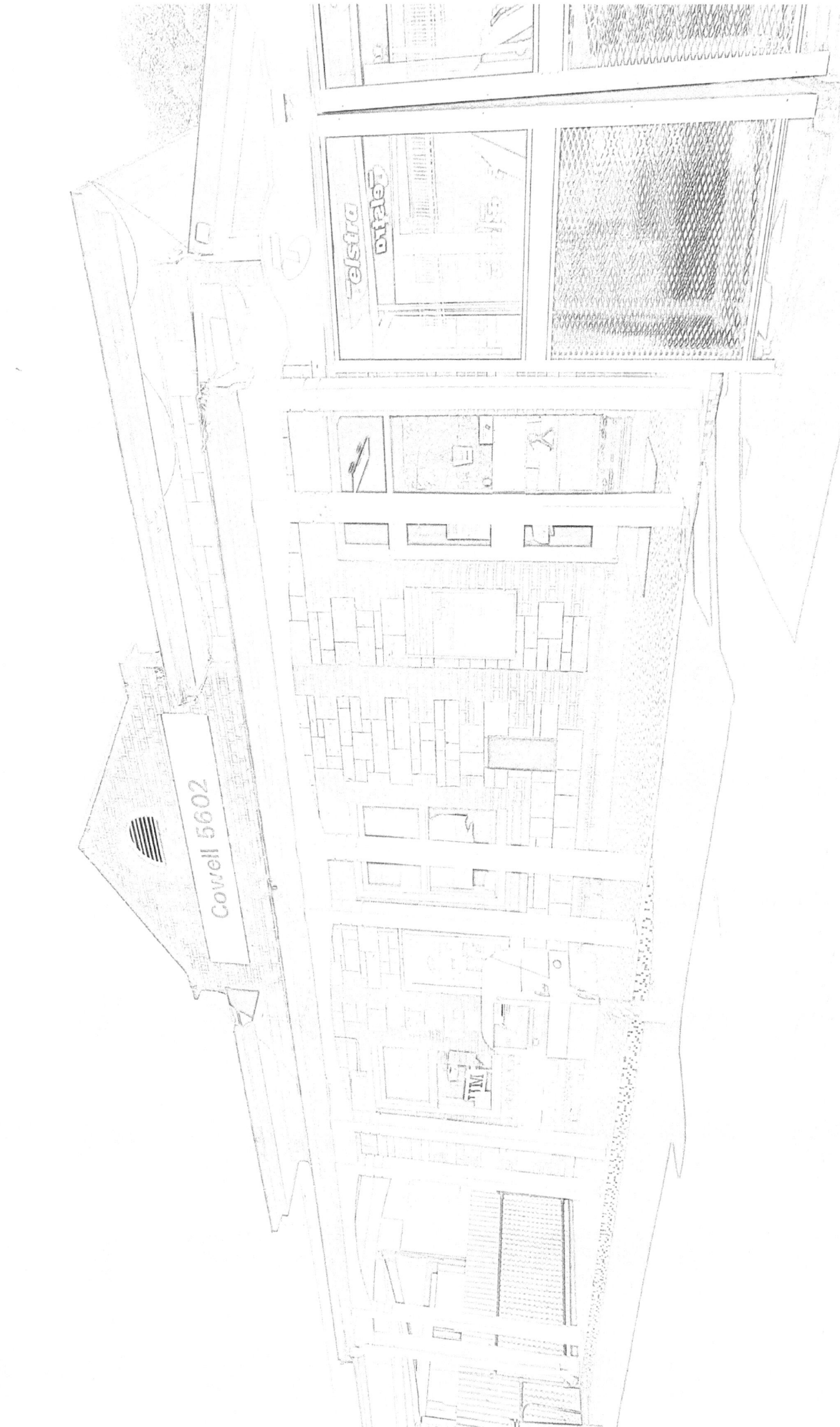

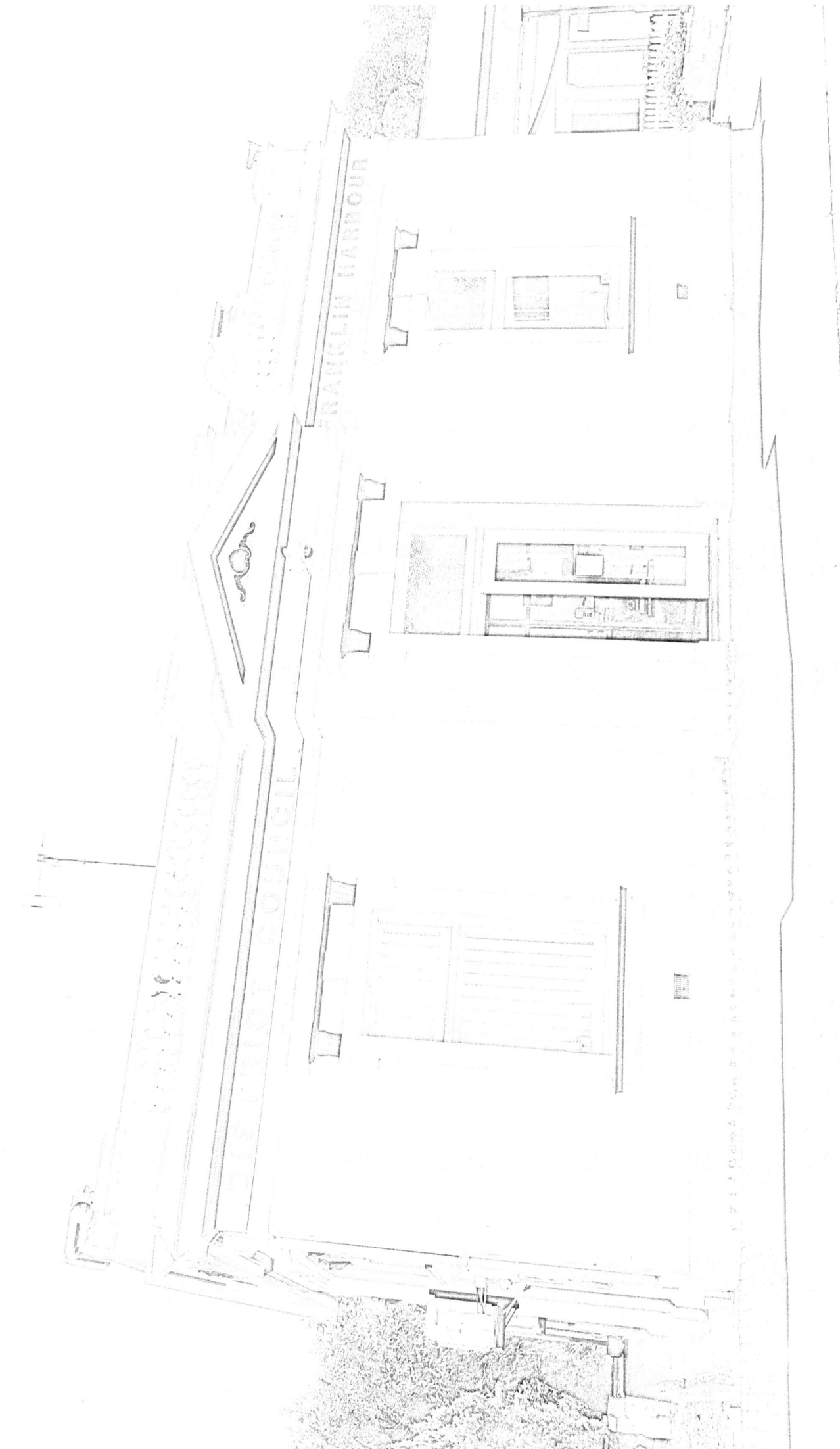

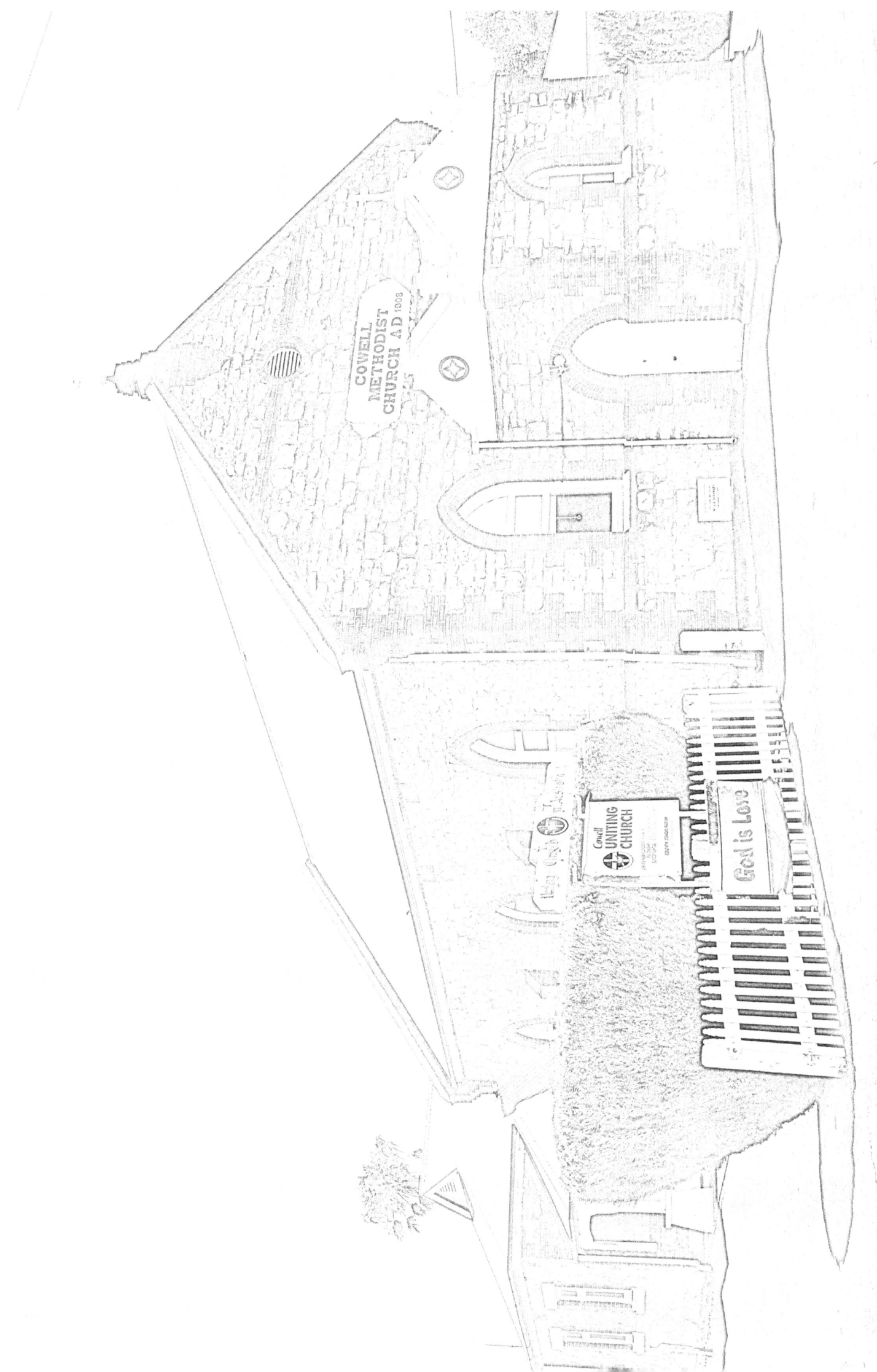

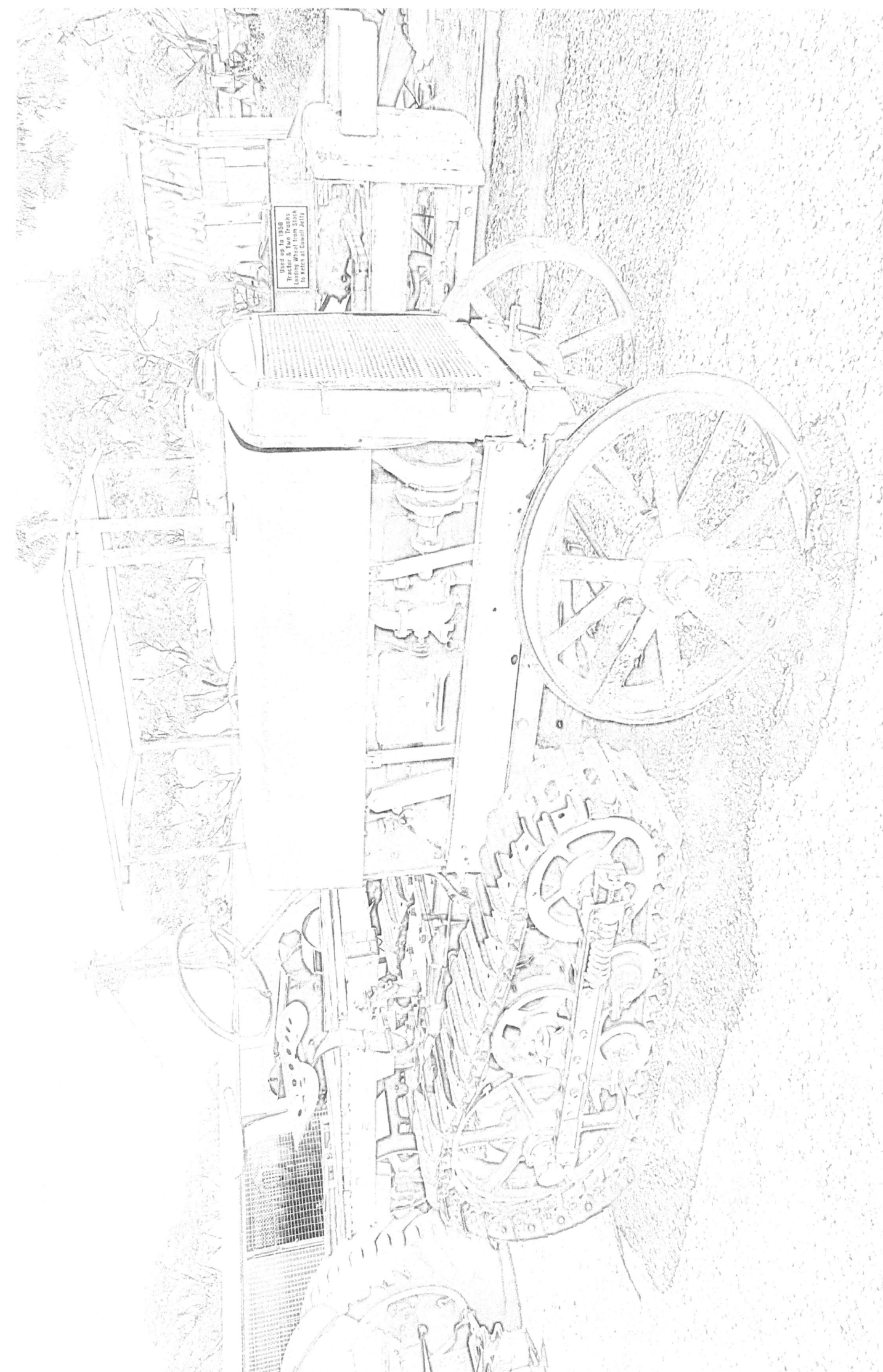

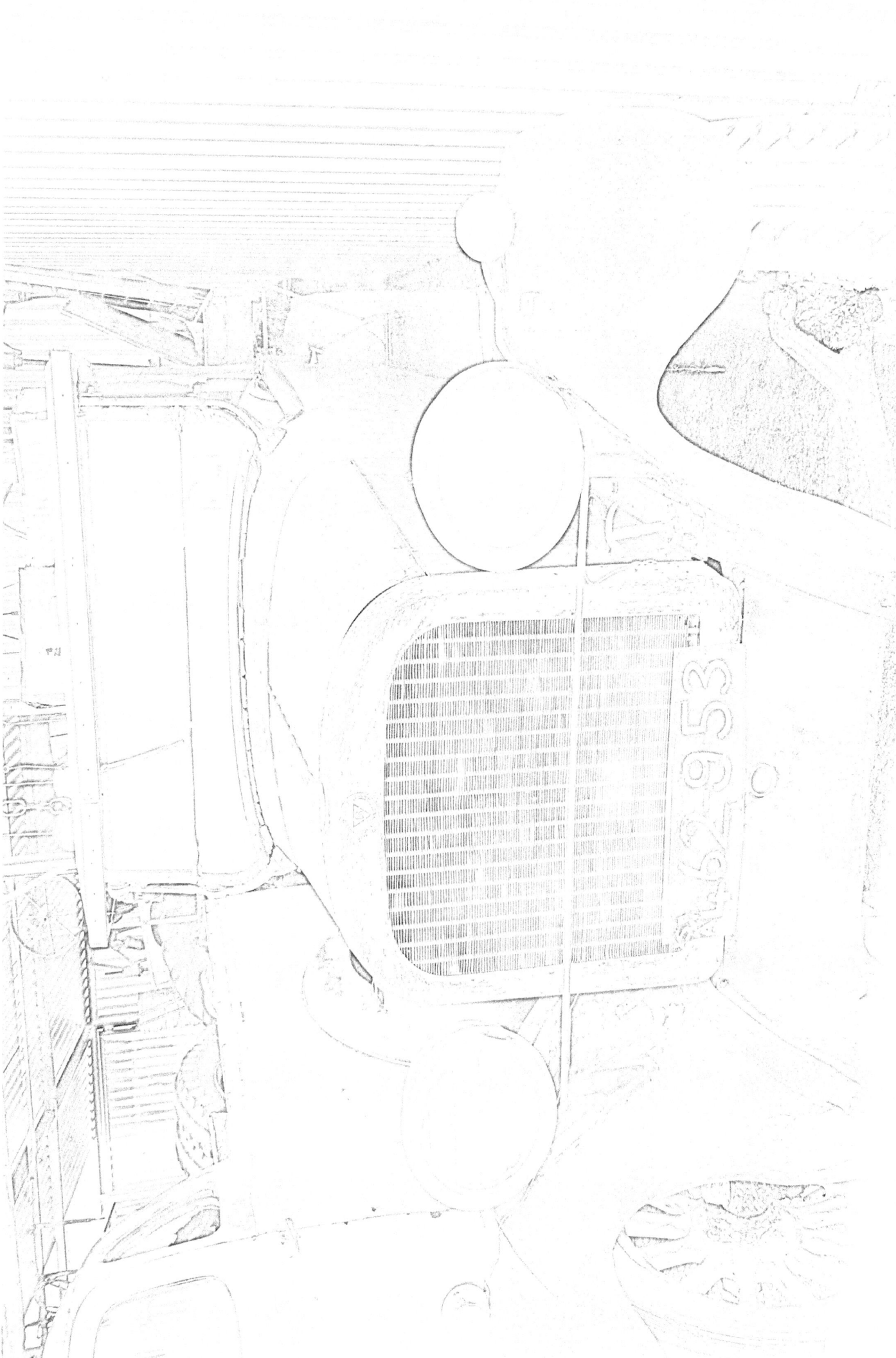

ARNO BAY

WAR MEMORIAL HALL INC.

1914 – 18

1939 – 45

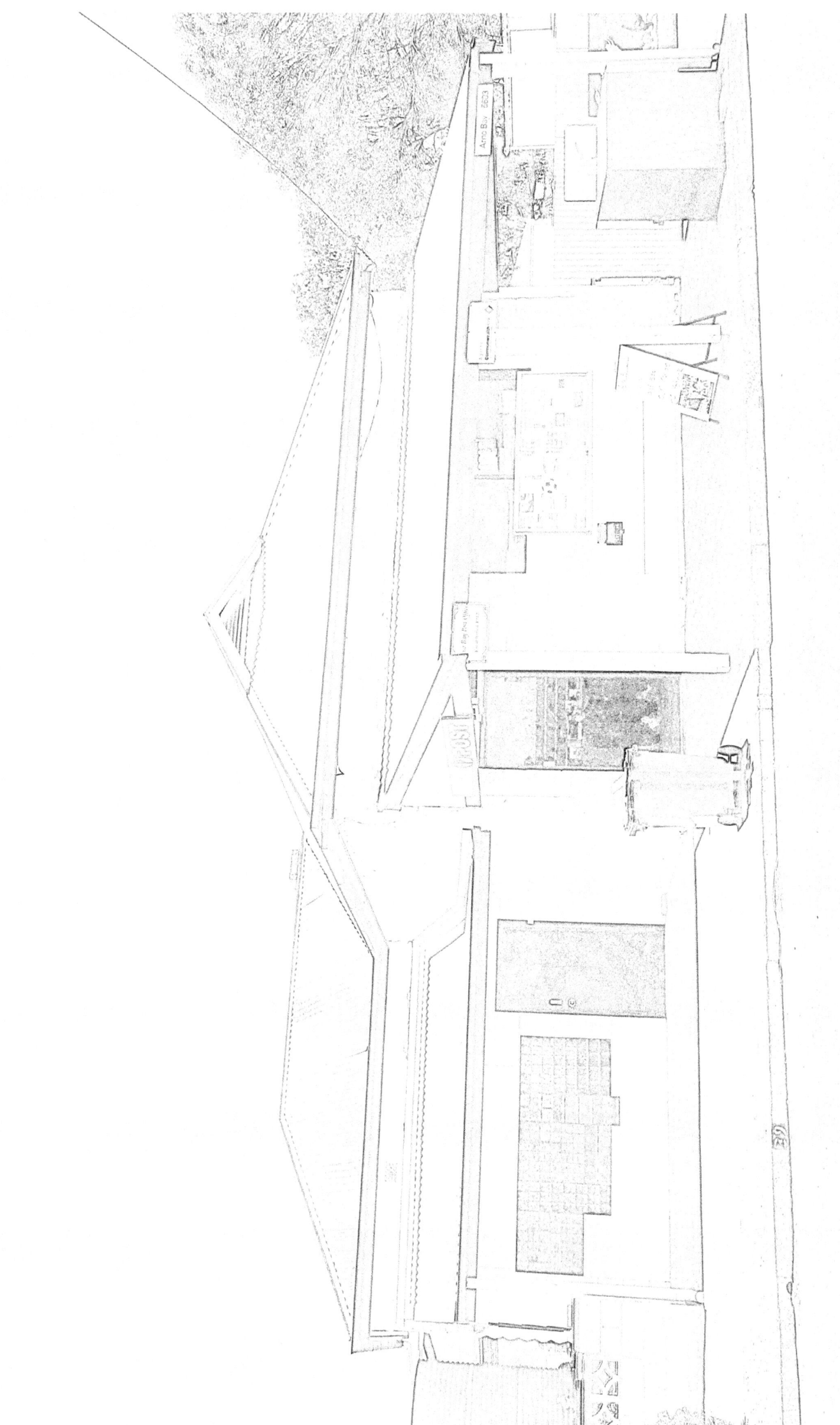

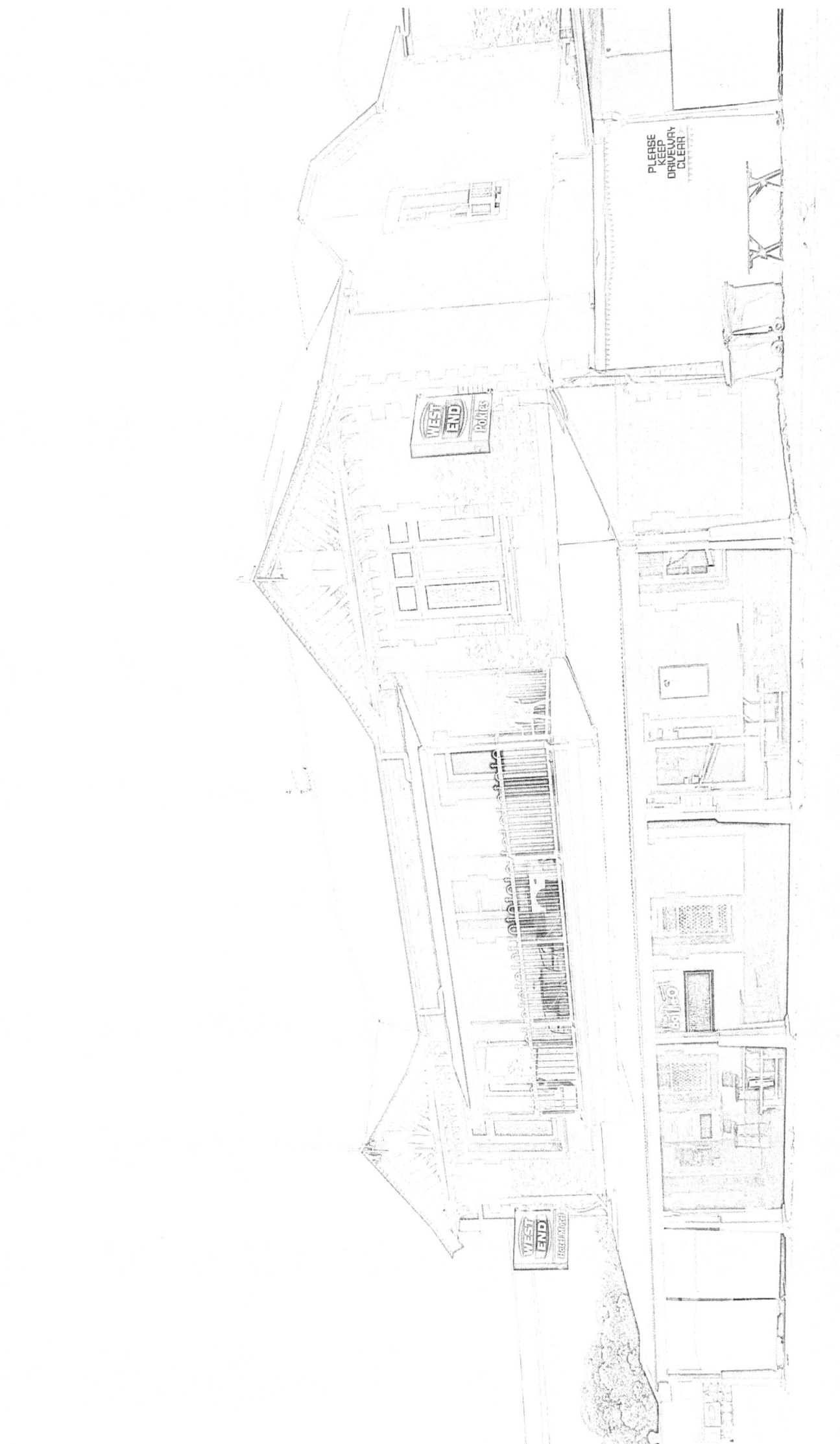

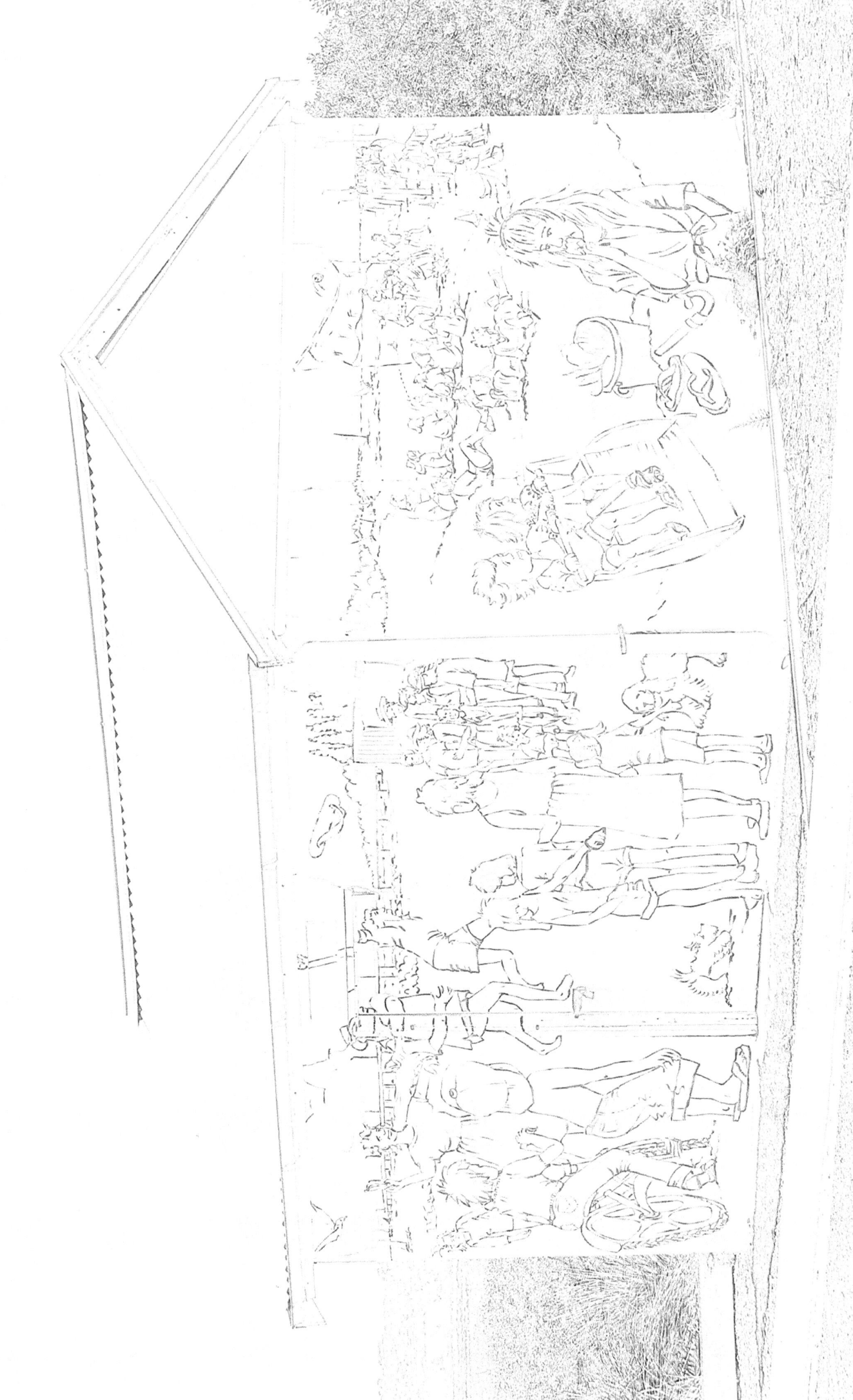

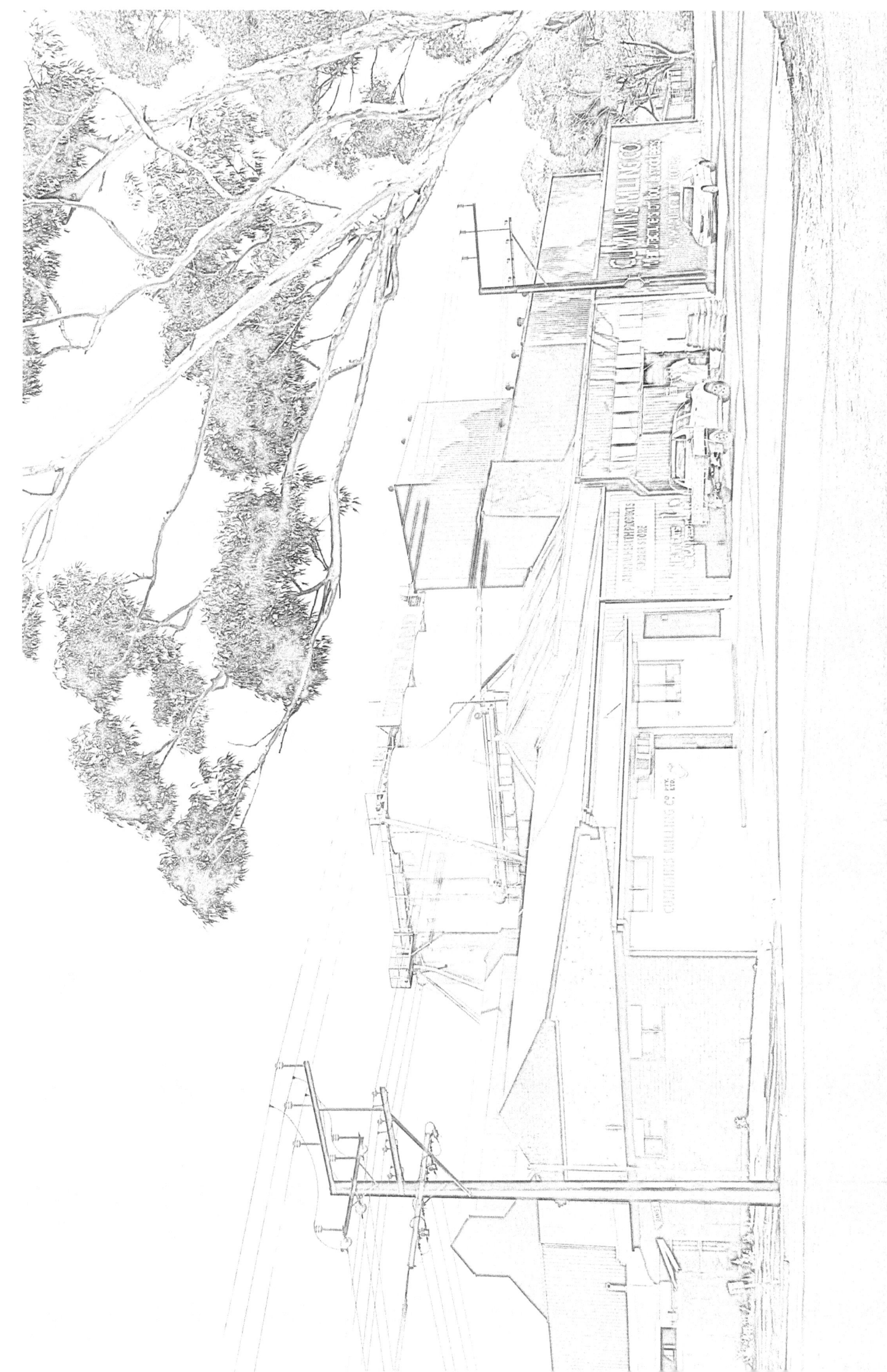

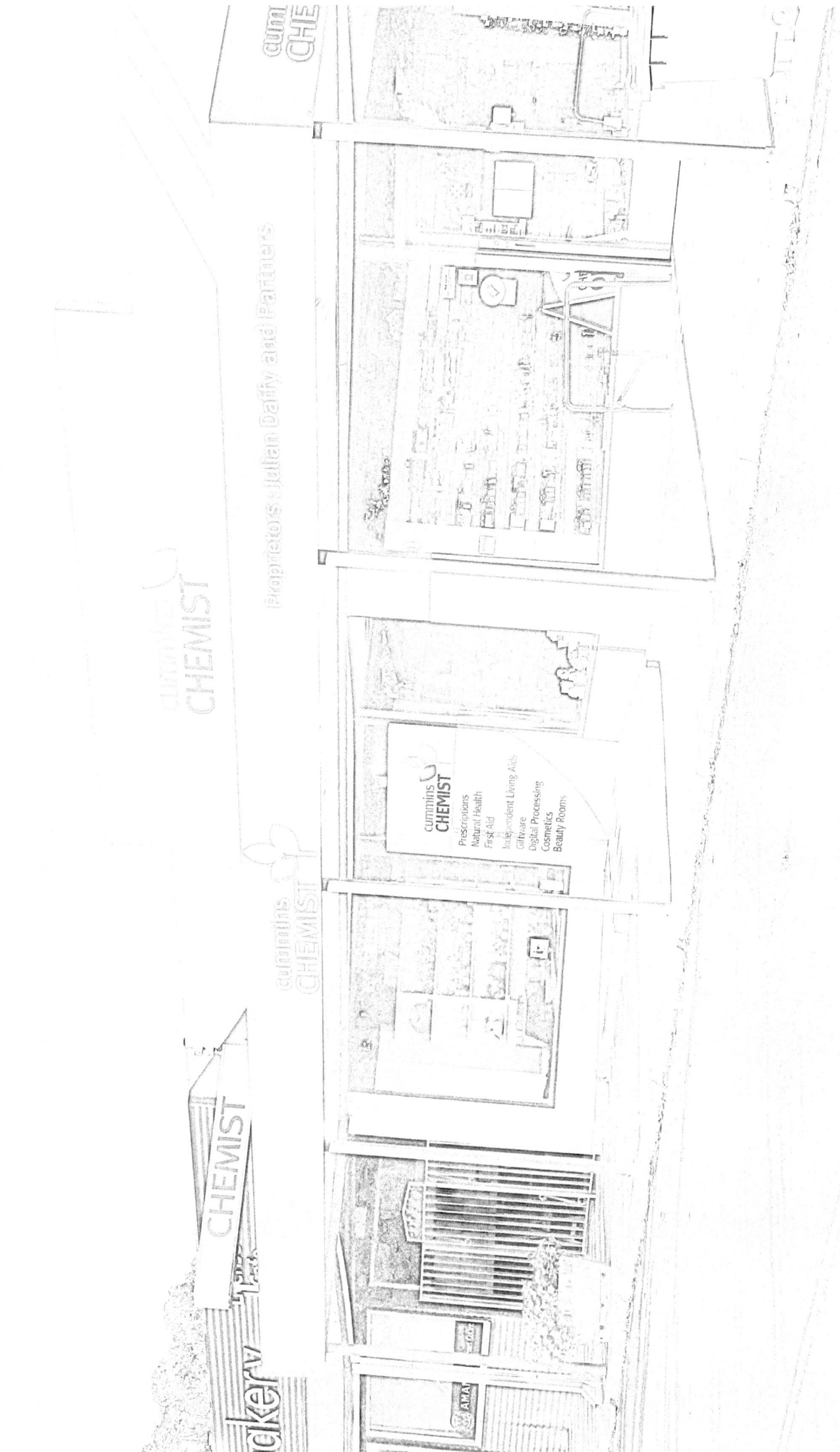

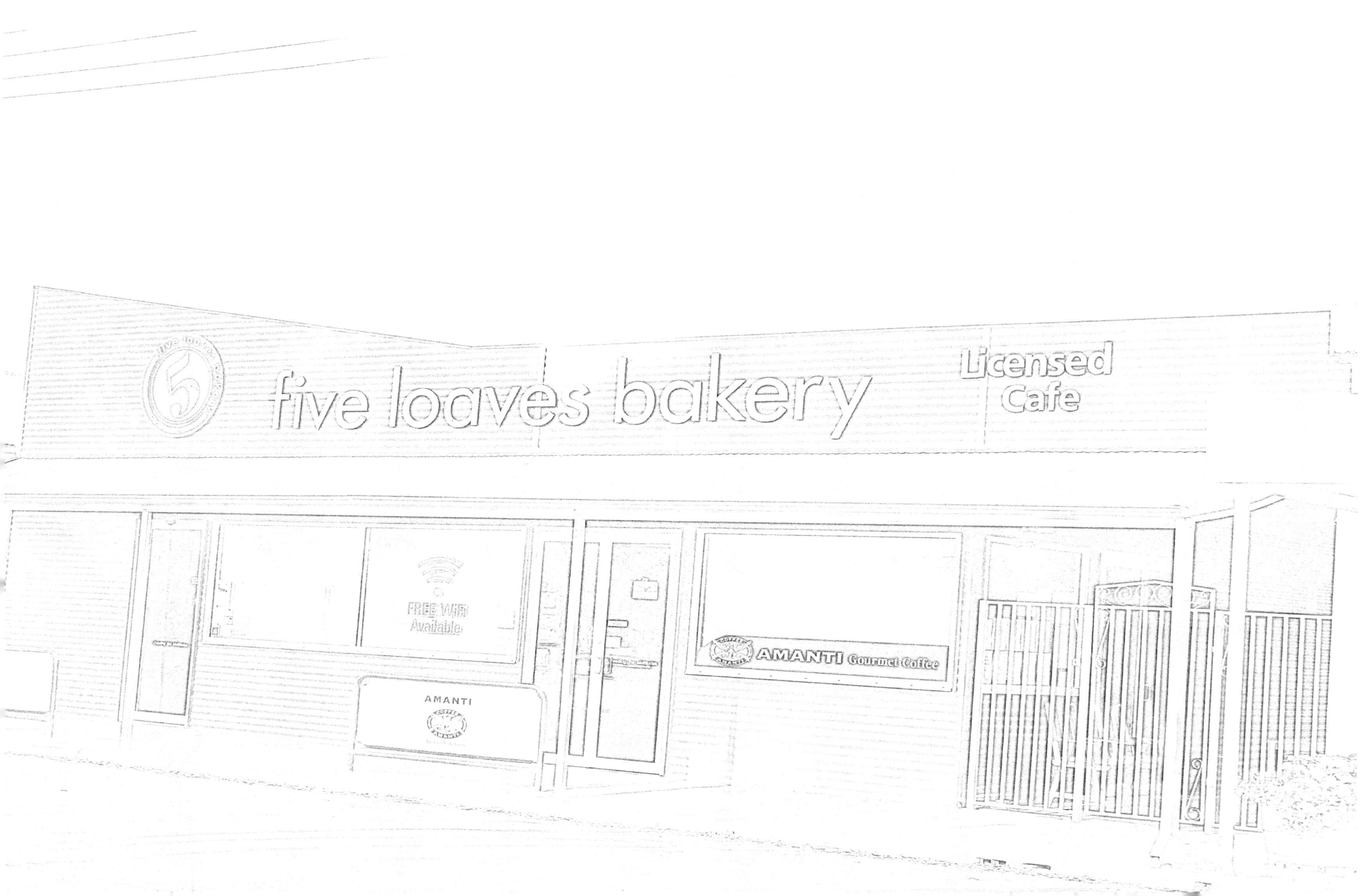

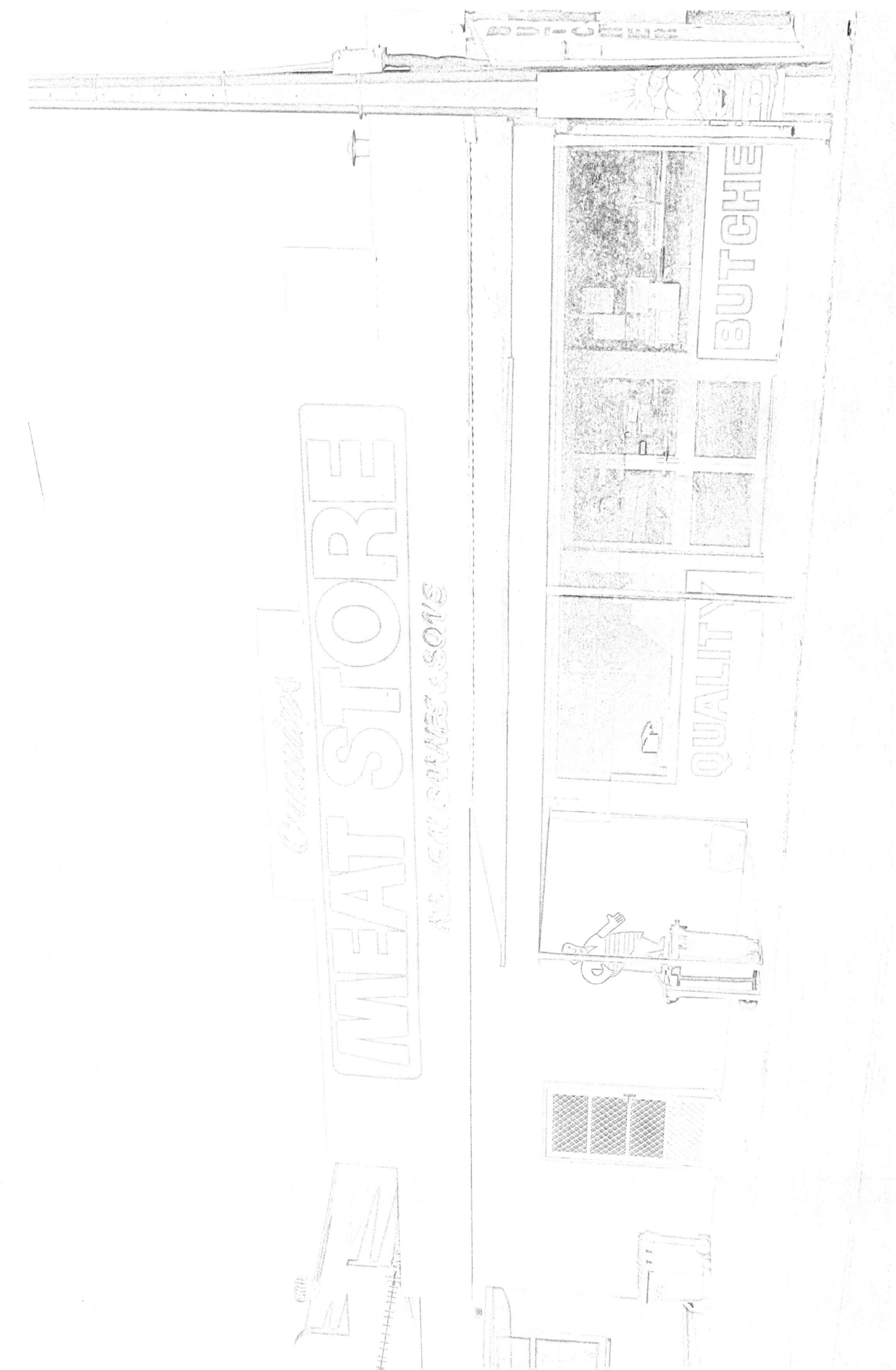

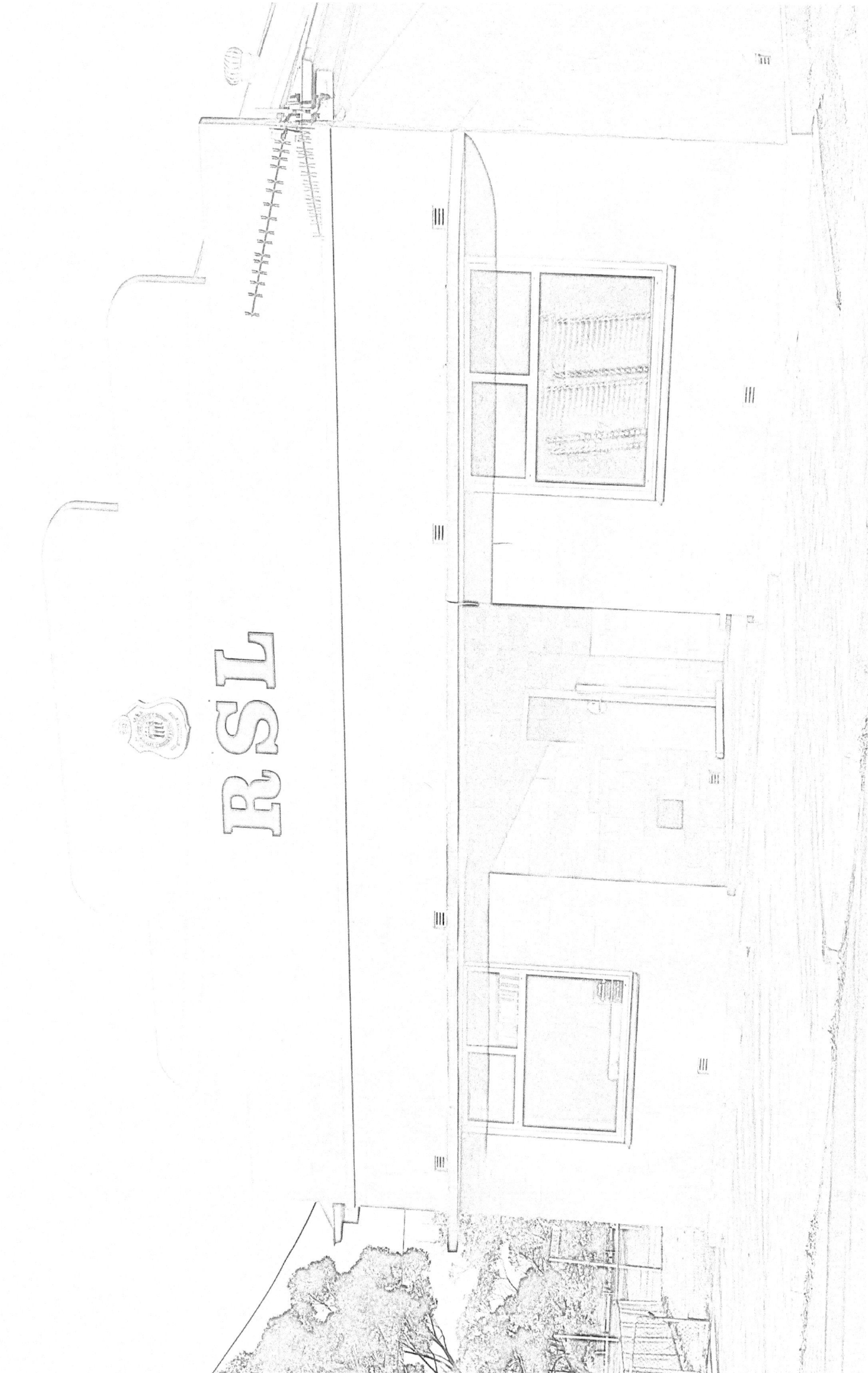

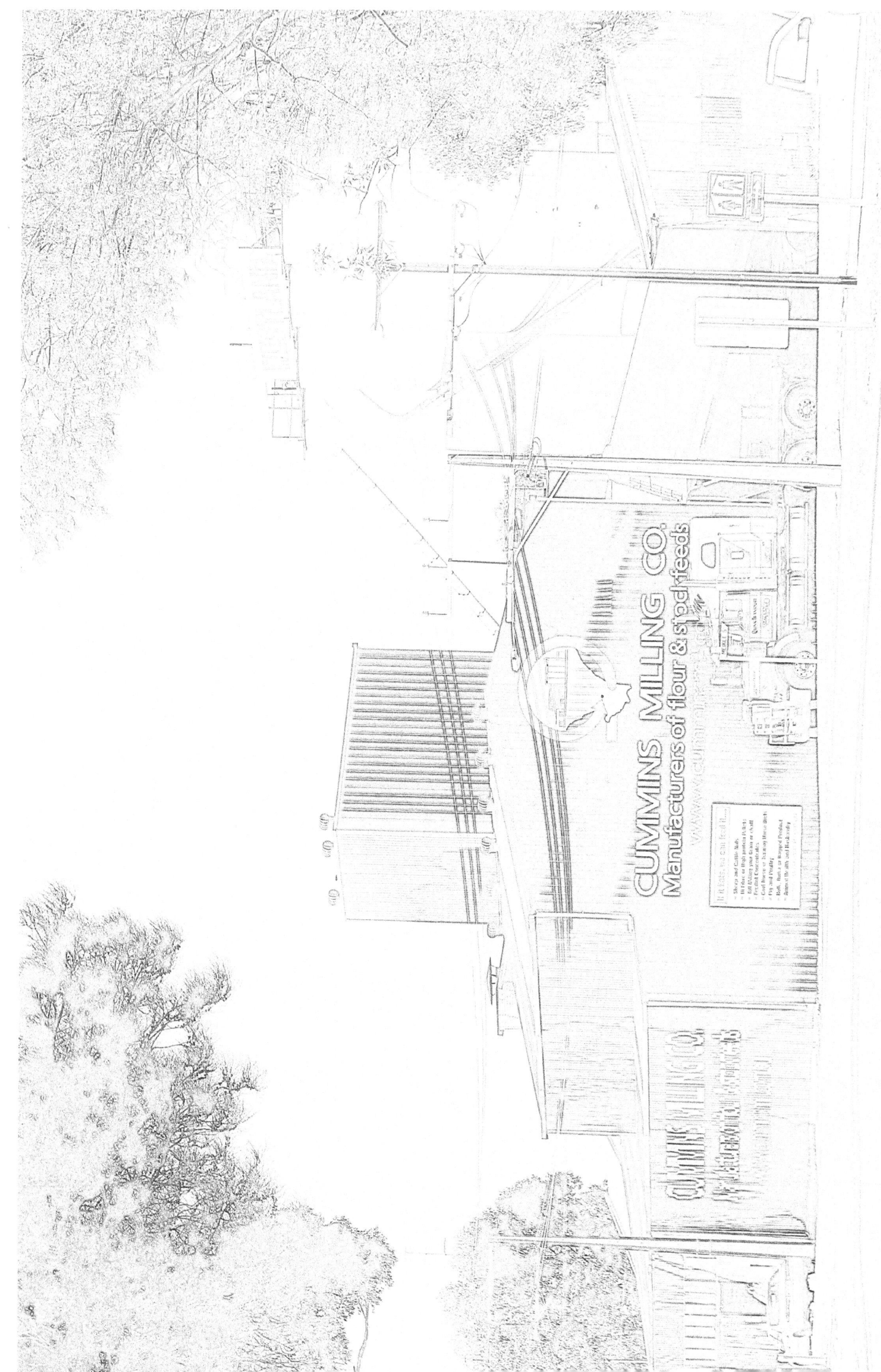

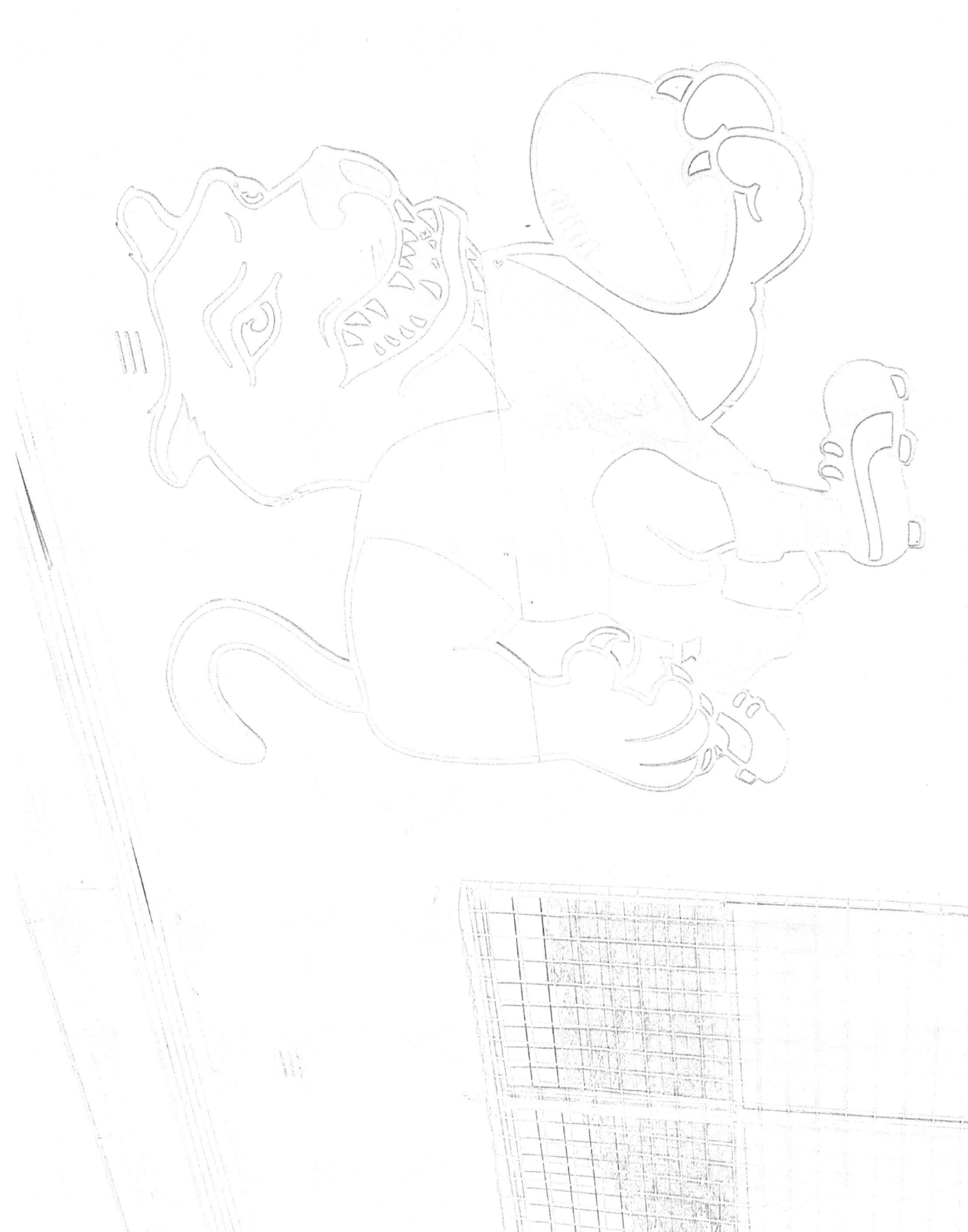

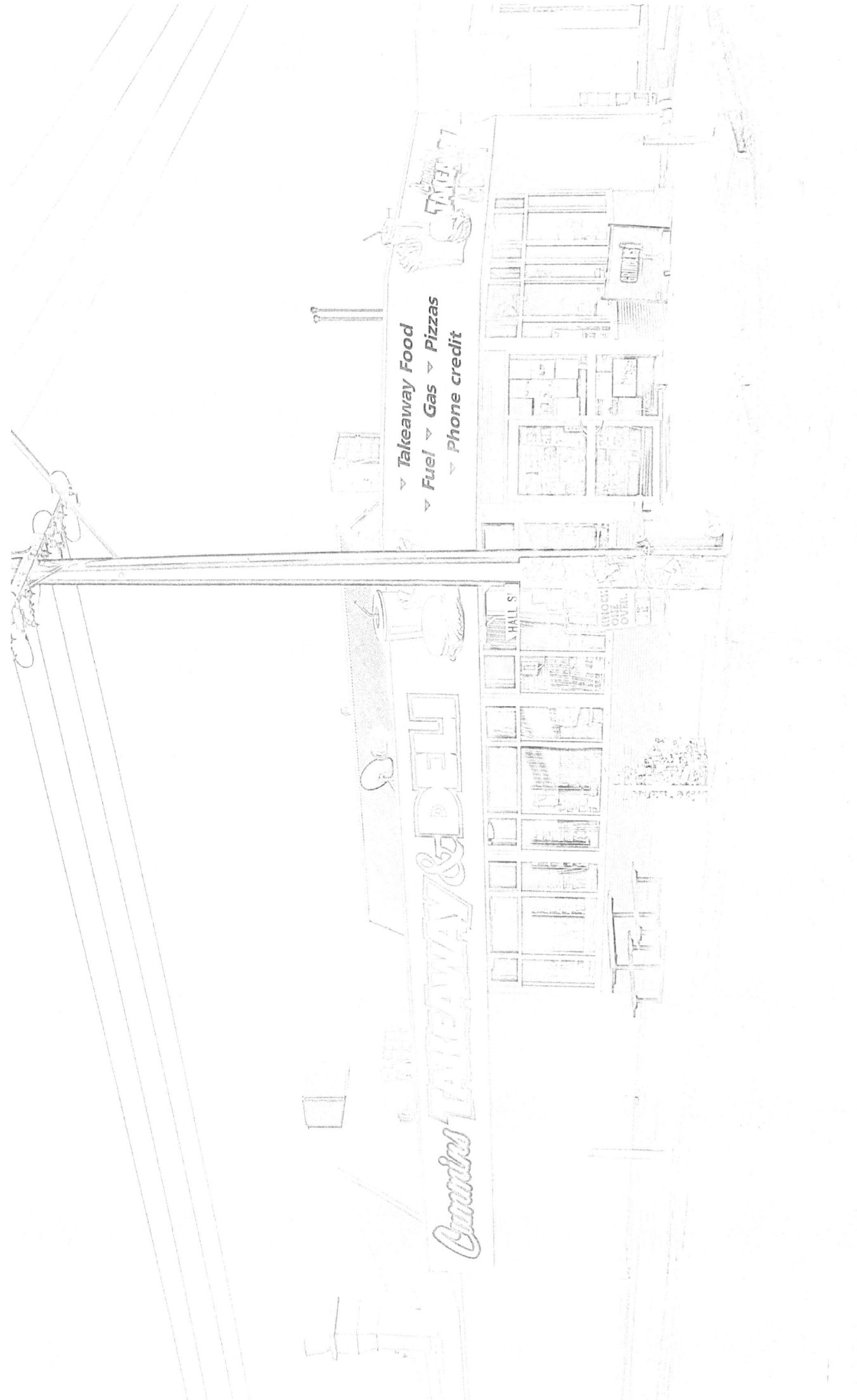

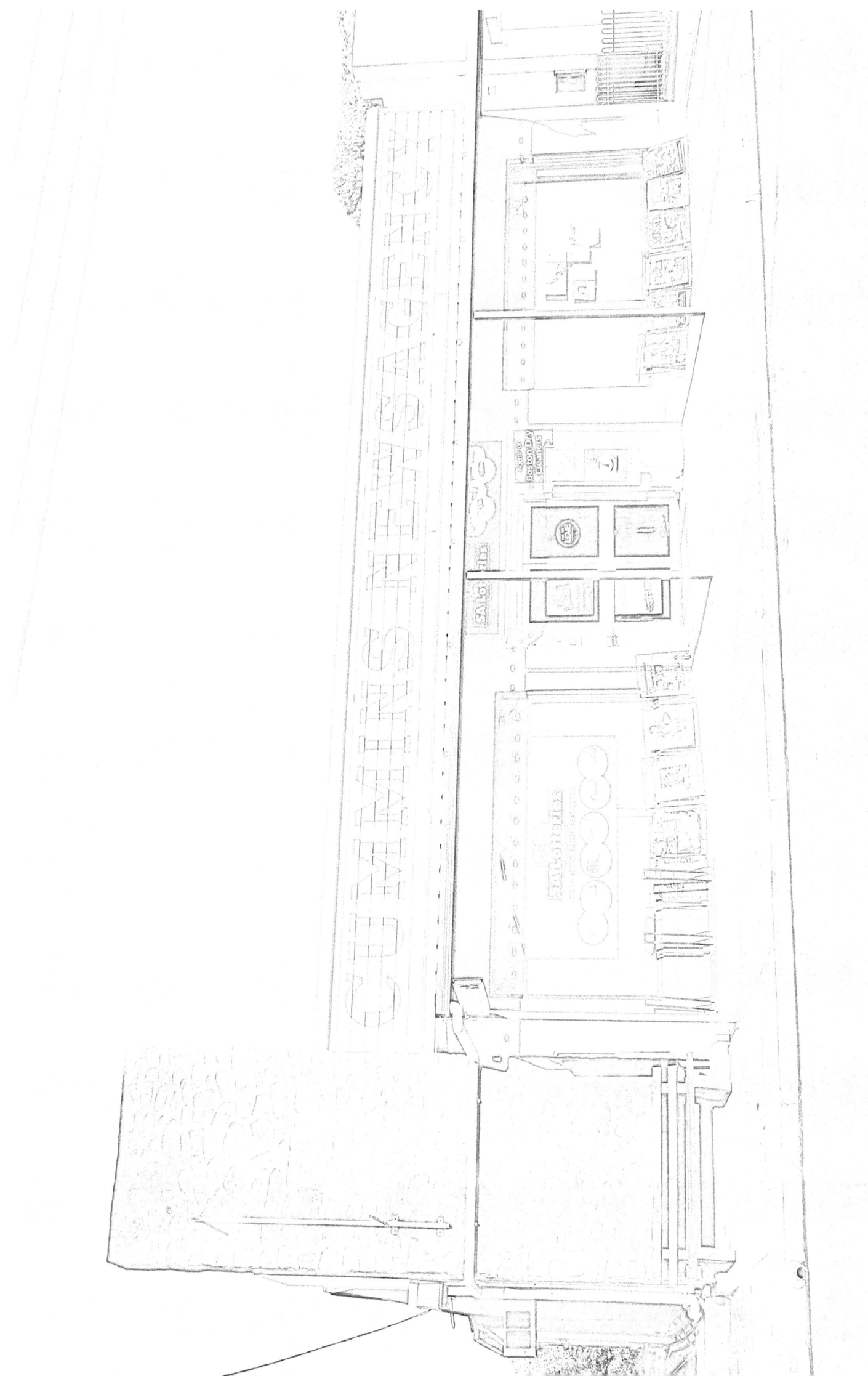

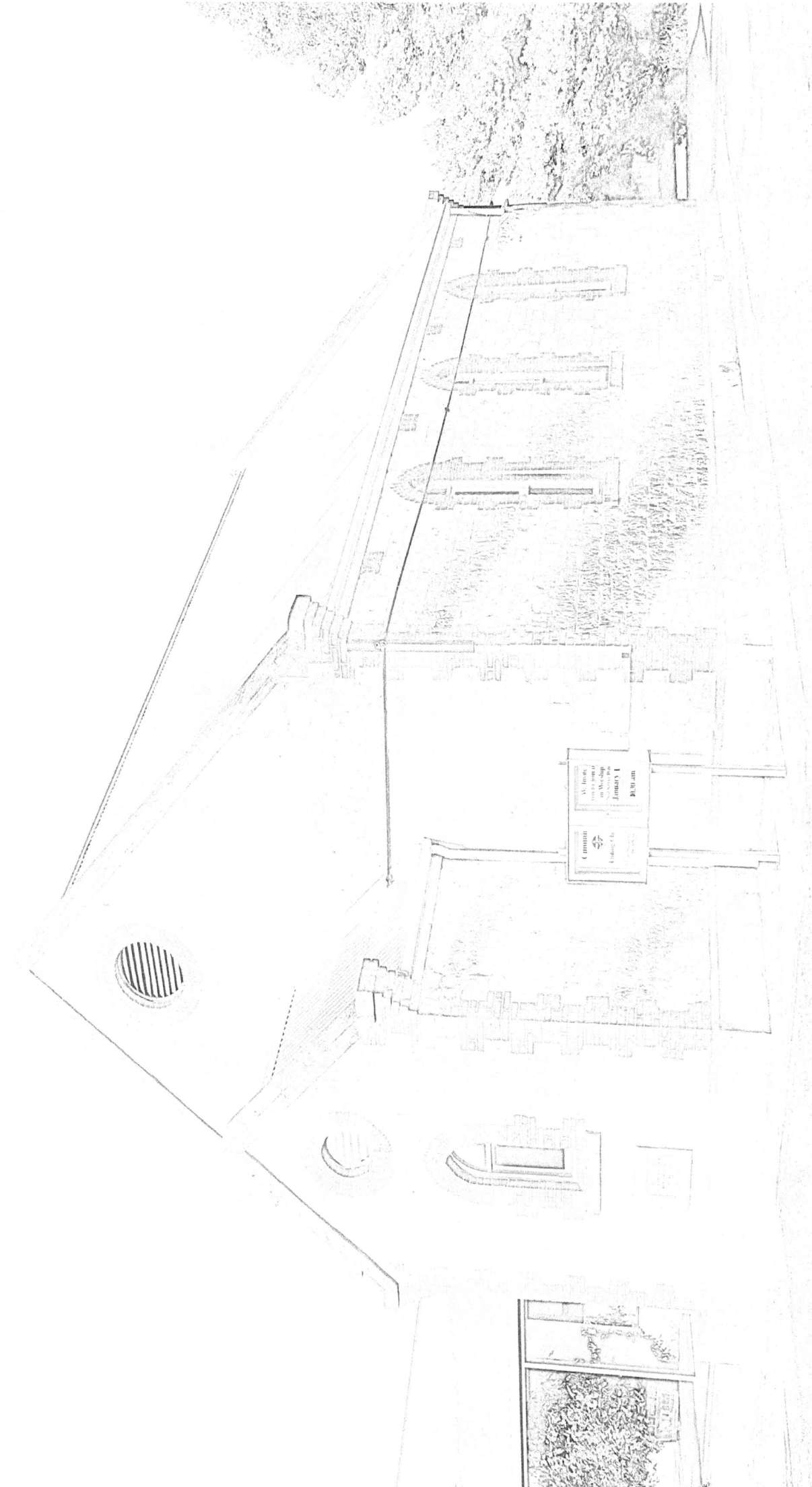

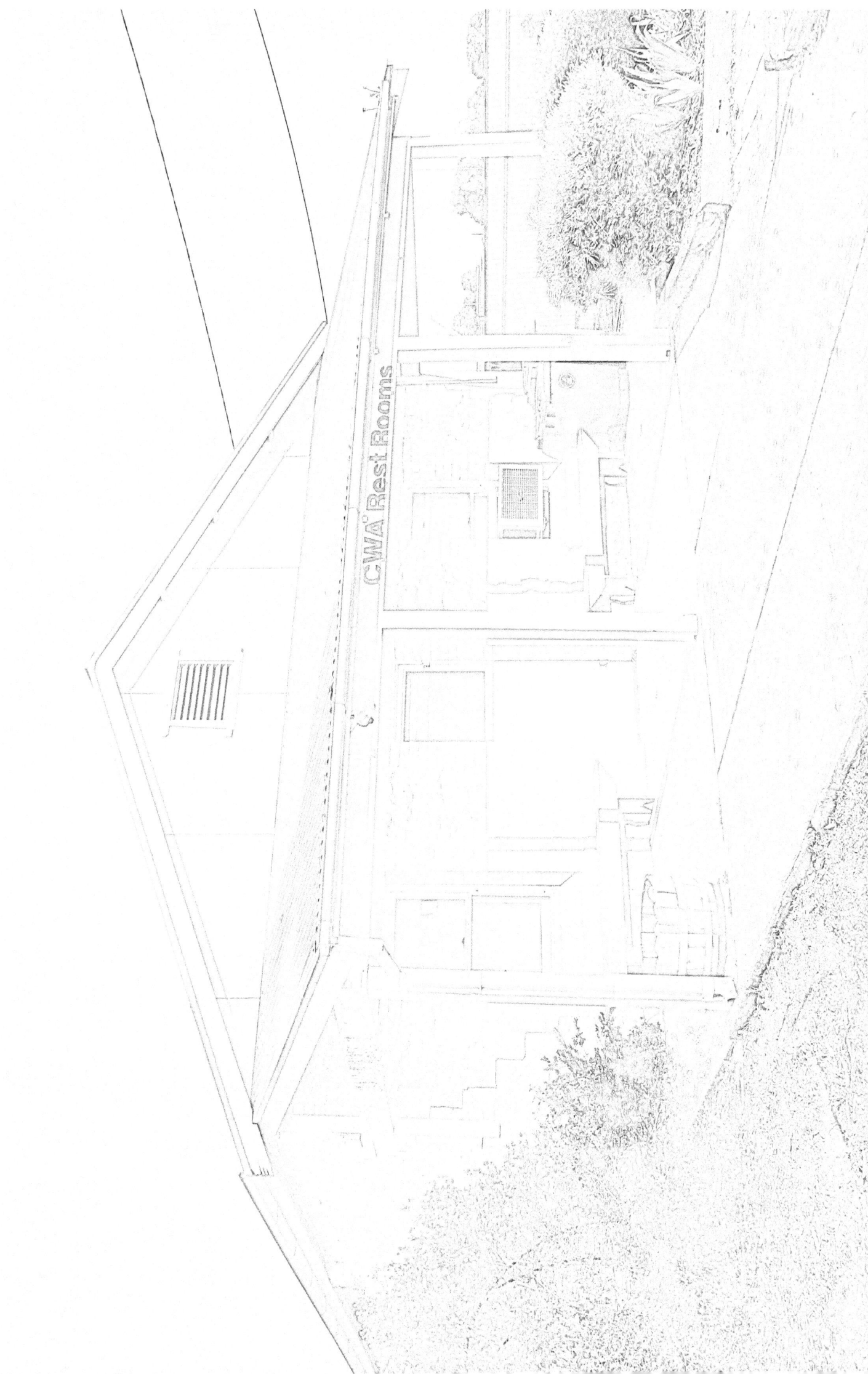

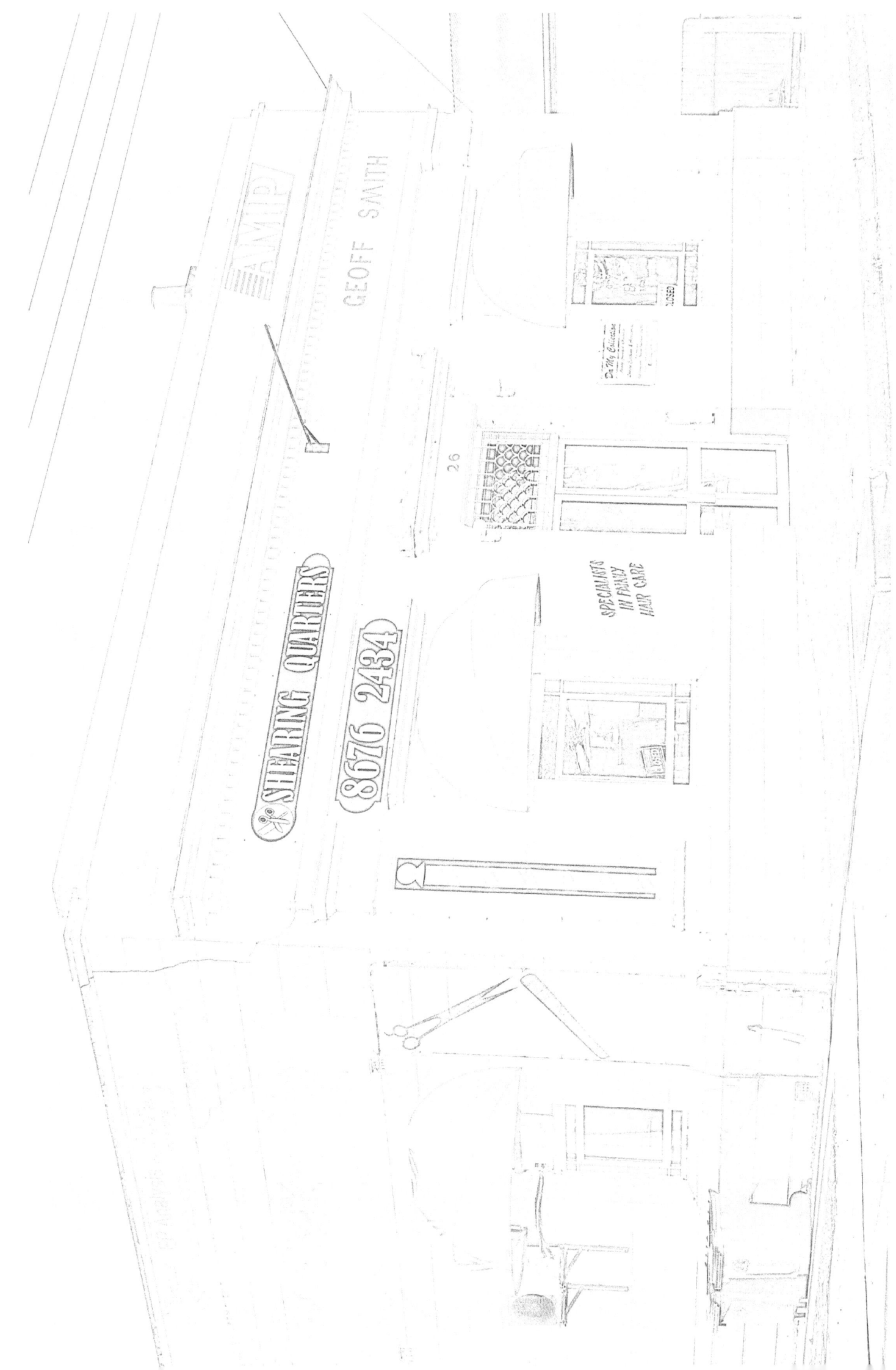

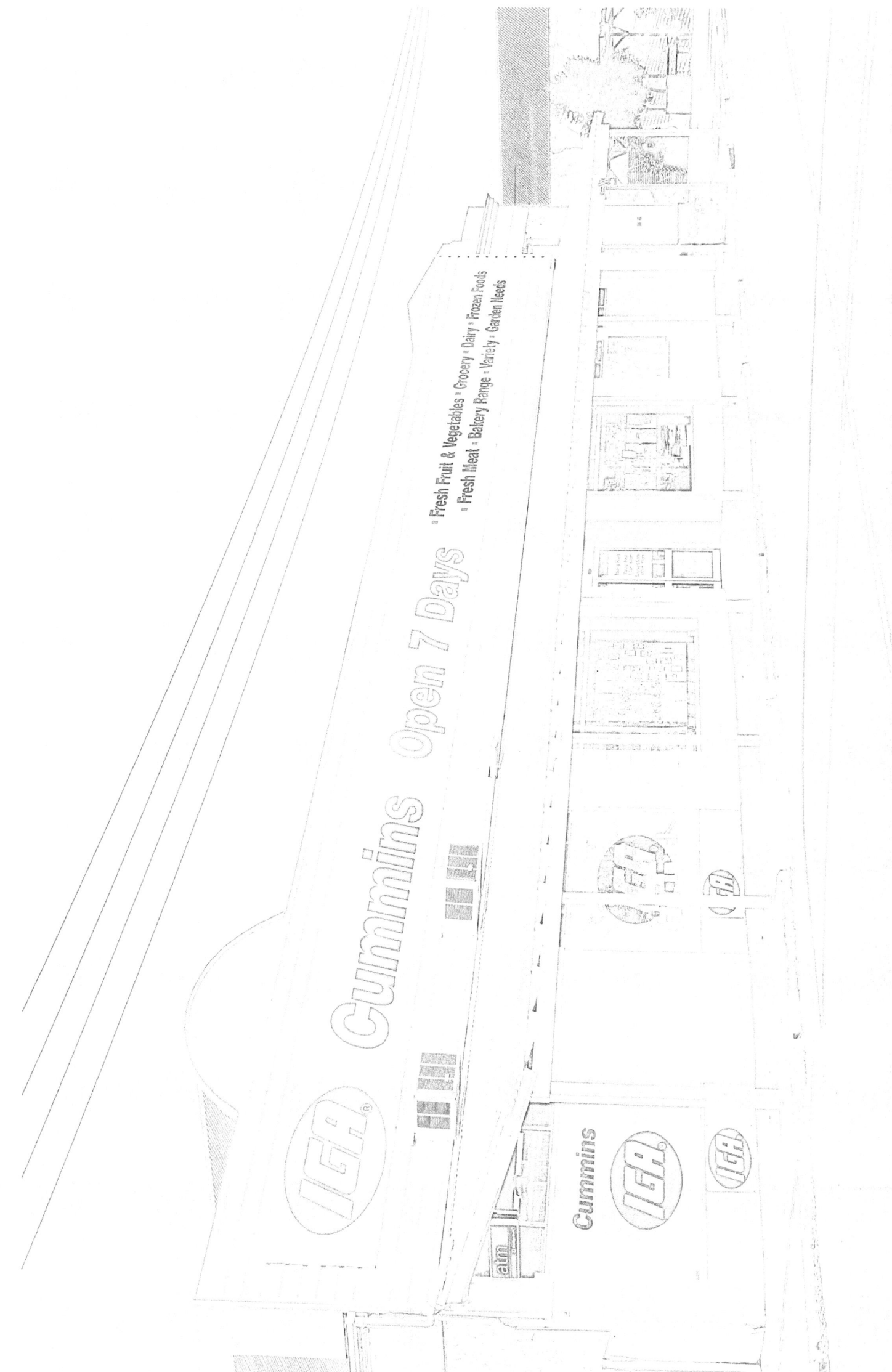

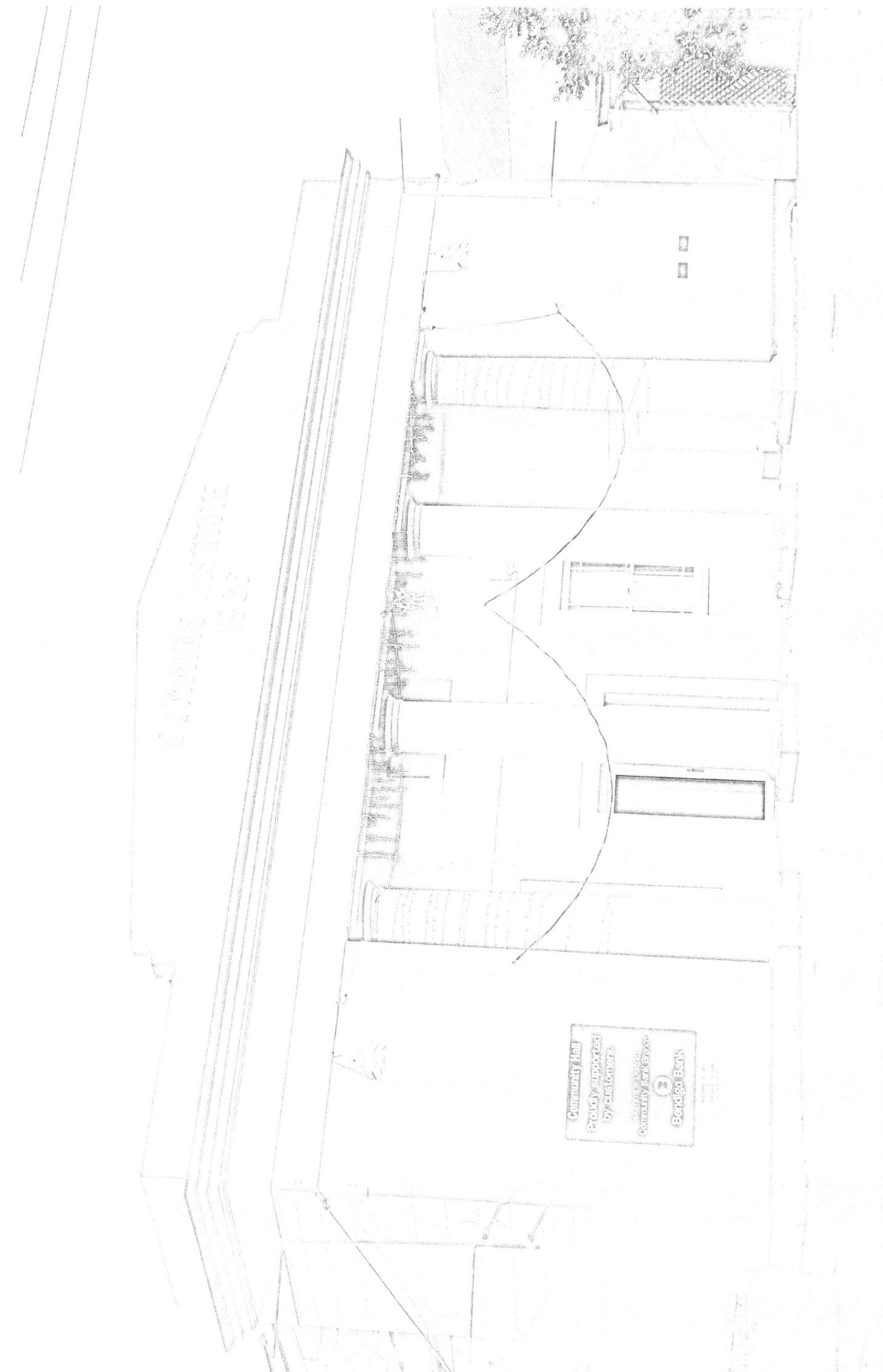

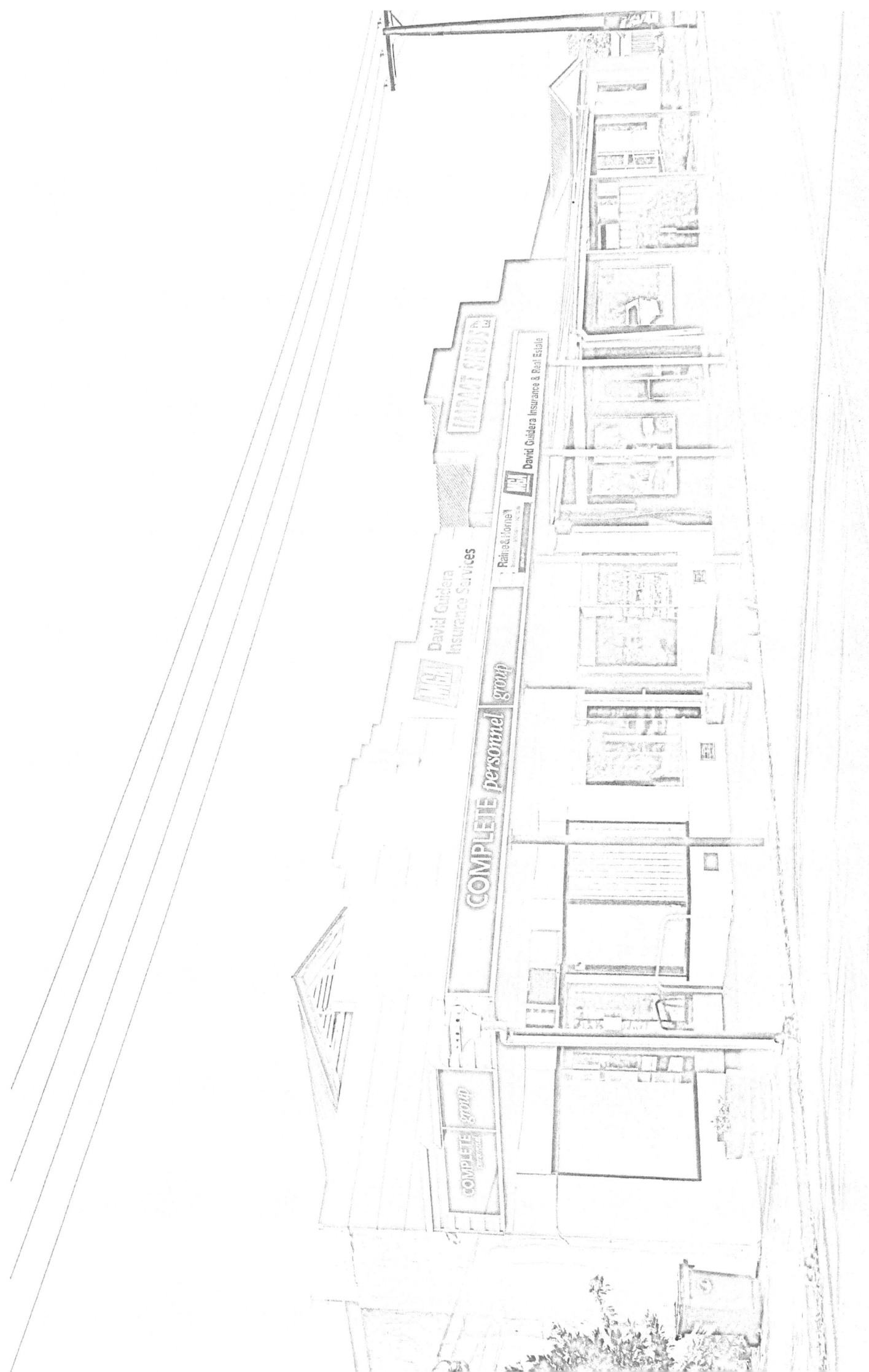

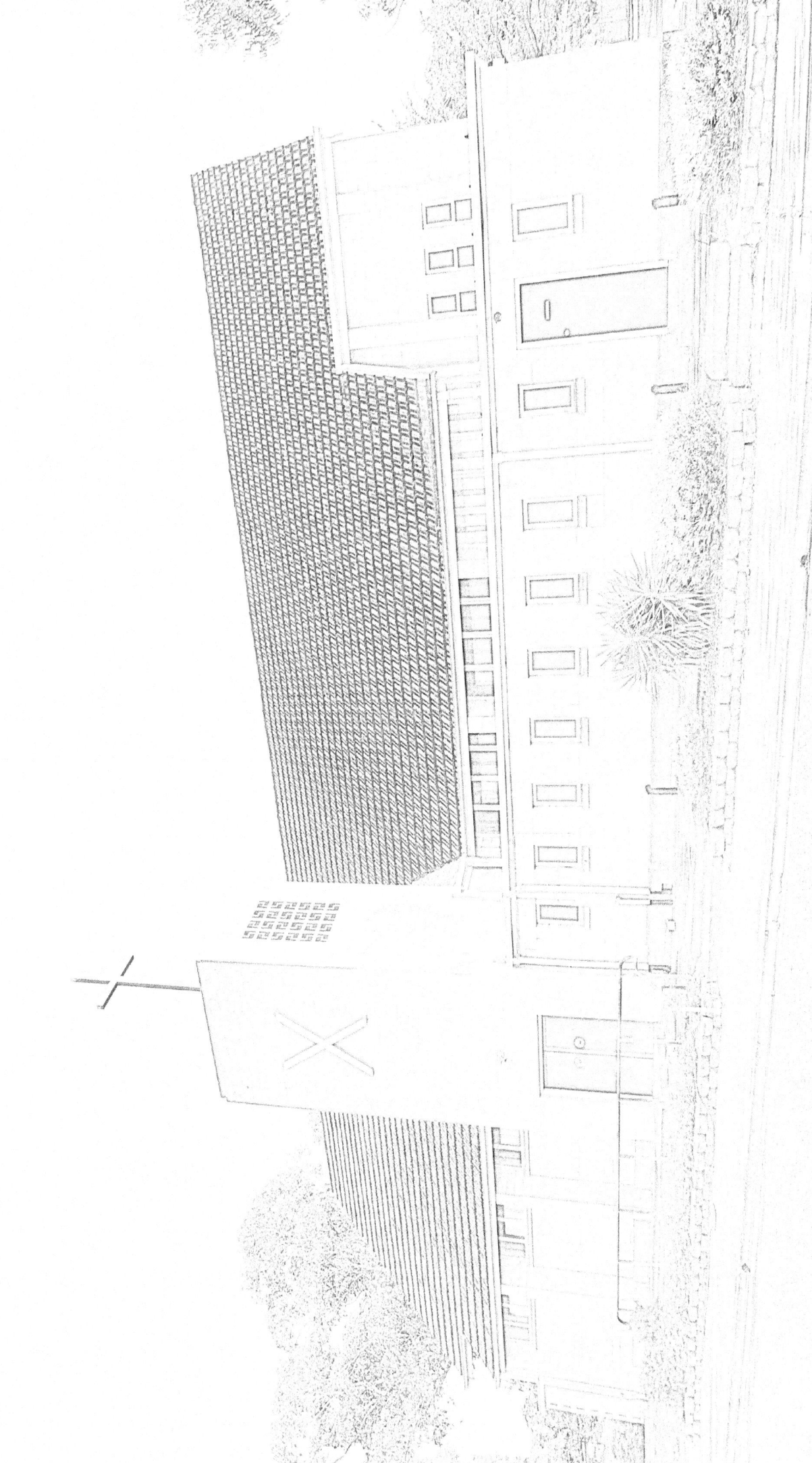

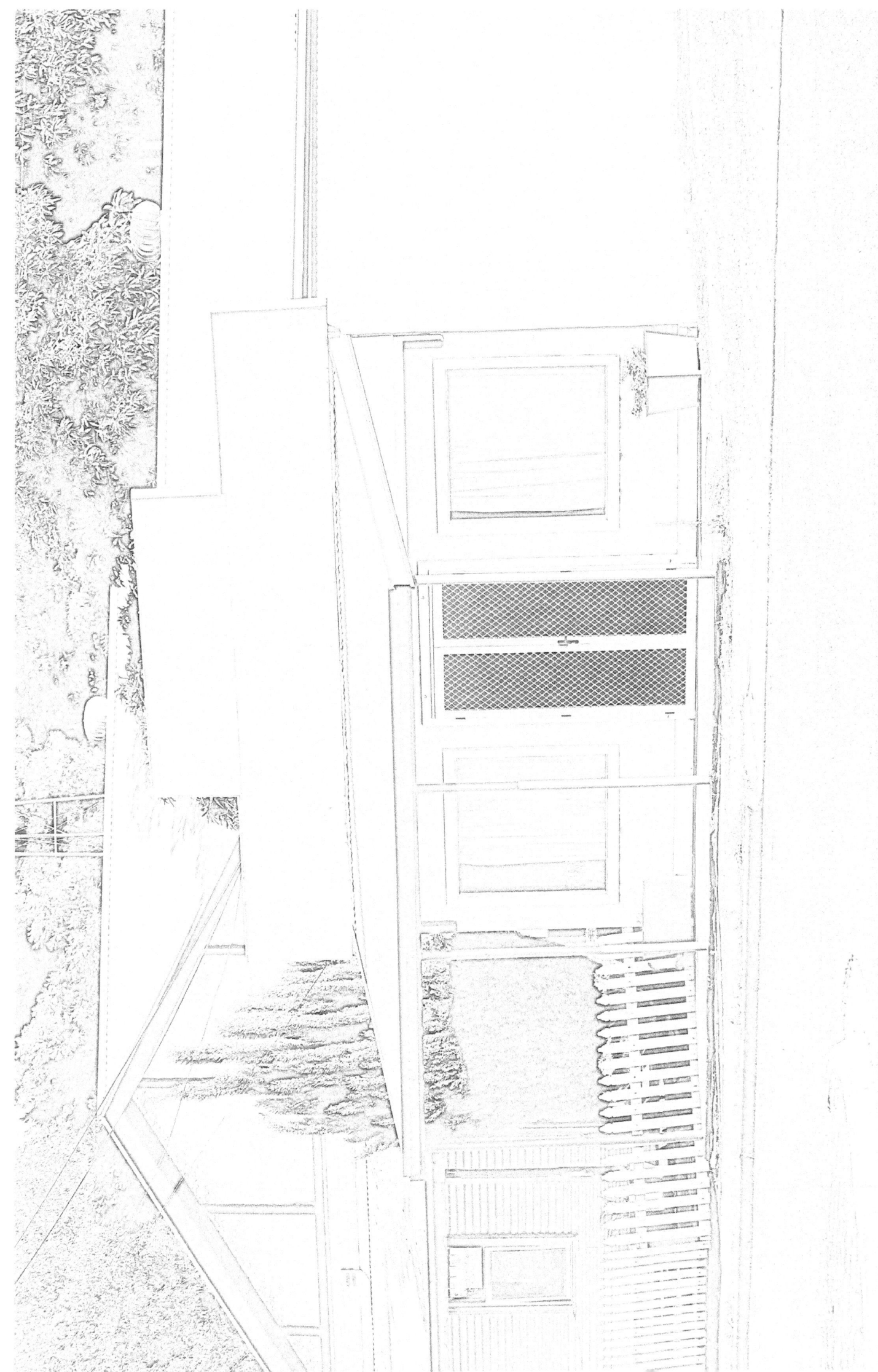

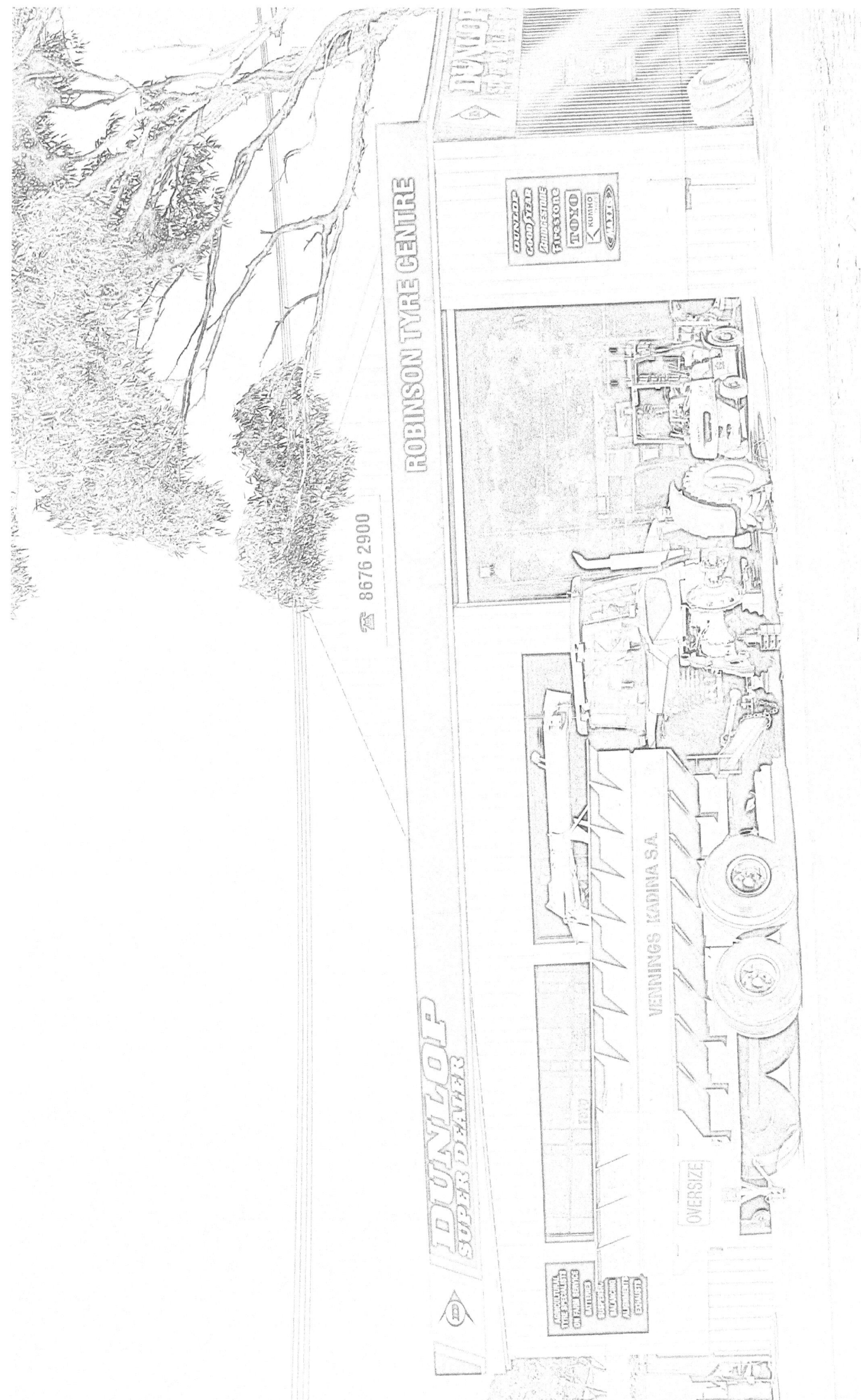

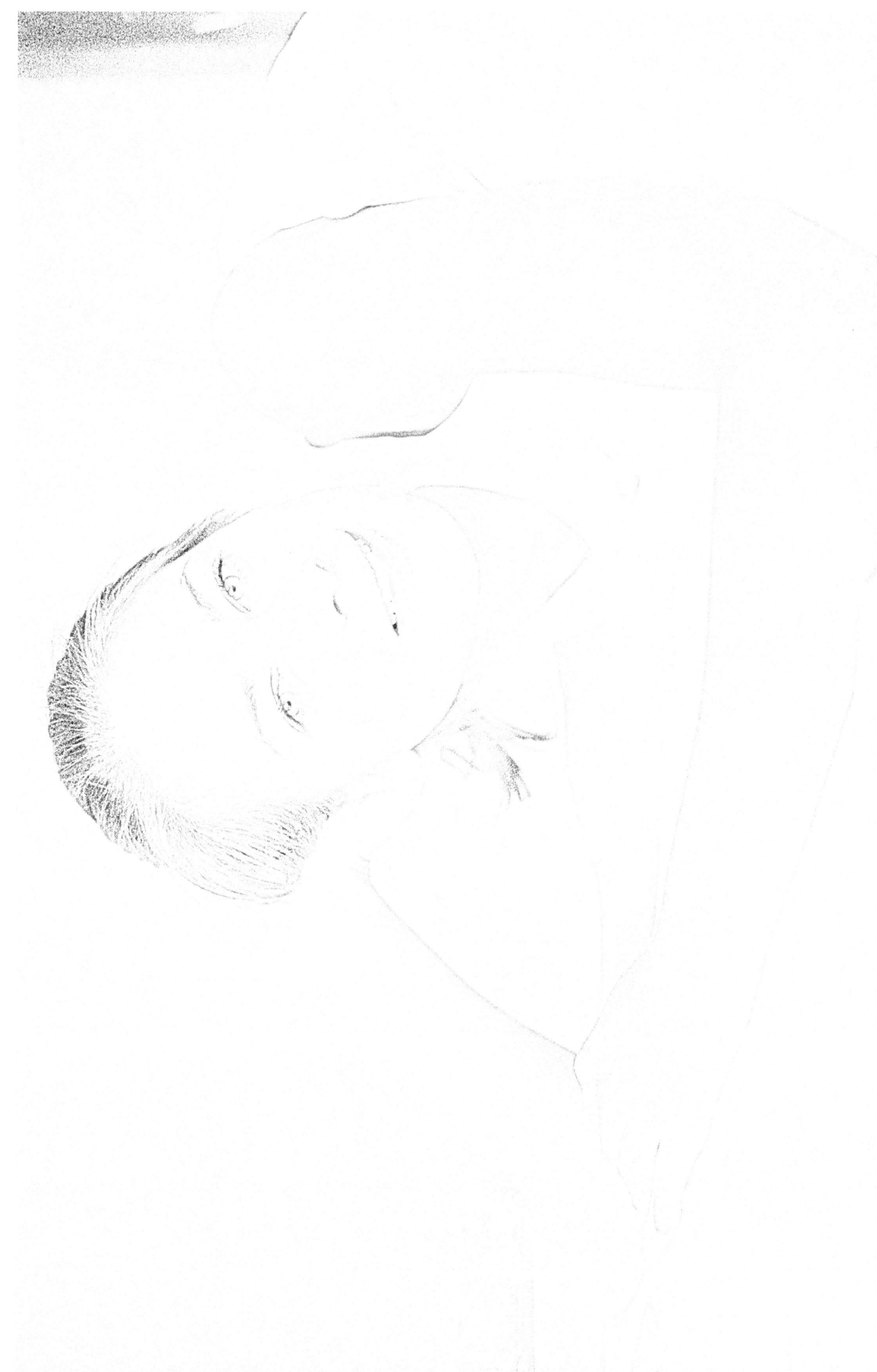